STUDENT LEADERSHIP UNIVERSITY
STUDY GUIDE SERIES

8 ESSENTIALS FOR A LIFE OF SIGNIFICANCE

JAY STRACK

RON LUCE

NELSON IMPACT
A Division of Thomas Nelson Publishers
Since 1798

www.thomasnelson.com

Published by Nelson Impact, a Division of Thomas Nelson, Inc., P.O. Box 141000, Nashville, TN 37214.

All Scripture quotations are taken from *The New King James Version*®. Copyright © 1982 by Thomas Nelson, Inc. Used by permission. All rights reserved.

ISBN 1-4185-0598-6

Printed in the United States of America

06 07 08 RRD 9 8 7 6 5 4 3 2 1

Page design by Crosslin Creative
2743 Douglas Lane, Thompsons Station, Tennessee 37179

CONTENTS

INTRODUCTION

Life is either a daring adventure or nothing.

— Helen Keller

These pages tell incredible true stories of teens that lived in Bible times. You will be challenged, amazed, encouraged, and inspired by the stories of teens whose lives made a real impact in their world, including Daniel, David, Esther, Joseph, Timothy, and others. Granted, the world they lived in was different from the one you live in, but their challenges and temptations were the same.

Eight Essentials for a Life of Significance is designed to help you change the world around you by first implementing change in your own life. In this study guide, we will walk through the eight essentials that will transform your life. As God begins to work in your life, people will see the change in your attitude, behavior, and even in your conversation. You may find people asking, *What's different about you? Can I get in on that?*

Then, as you begin to partner with others who believe and live as you do, you will be able to boldly move forward with the dreams God has set before you and to go about making a real difference in your world—in your school, in your home, and in your church.

This is not just a study to read through; it is a book to do. Open your heart to what God has to say to you and you will find new meaning in your life—a bold courageous faith, a quiet inner peace, and a passion for going above and beyond.

KEY

STUDENT LEADERSHIP UNIVERSITY CURRICULUM

Throughout this study guide, you will see several icons or headings that represent an idea, a statement, or a question that we want you to consider as you experience Scripture in this study guide series. Refer to the descriptions below to help you remember what the icons and headings mean.

transfuse (trans FYOOZ)', to cause to pass from one to another; transmit

The goal of the lesson for the week.

Experience Scripture: Learning to really experience Scripture is the key element to "getting" who God is and all that He has in store for you.

infuse (in FYOOZ)', to cause to be permeated with something (as a principle or quality) that alters usually for the better

Through journaling, group discussion, and personal study, experience Scripture as it permeates your heart and alters your life.

Future Tense Living: Your choices today will determine your future. Learn how to live with dynamic purpose and influence.

Attitude Reloaded: Rethink your attitude! Learn to replace self-centered, negative, or limited thoughts with positive, courageous, compassionate thoughts that are based on God's unlimited ability and power.

 In His Steps: Every attitude and action of your life should begin with the questions, How would Jesus respond to this person and situation before me? What would He choose to do?

diffuse (di FYOOZ)︐ to pour out and permit or cause to spread freely; to extend, scatter

Once God's Word is infused into your heart, it will pour forth to others without restraint. In this section, explore what that looks like in your daily life.

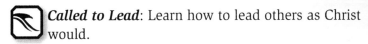 *Called to Lead*: Learn how to lead others as Christ would.

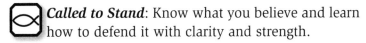 *Called to Stand*: Know what you believe and learn how to defend it with clarity and strength.

Called to Share: Sharing truth and serving others are results of a transformed life. How can you share with others the awesome things you're learning?

One Thing: Consider ONE THING you can do this week to make a difference in your life and/or the life of another.

FUSE BOX

Power up for the week with this focused truth.

CHAPTER 1

KEEP A QUIET TIME

DANIEL

KEY SCRIPTURE

For whatever things were written before were written for our learning, that we through the patience and comfort of the Scriptures might have hope.

—Romans 15:4

COULD THIS BE YOU?

He could hear the members of his church scream, "Champ!" as he ran up and down the court. Some people might have thought the cheer was merely praise for the six-foot-nine guy wearing the L.A. Lakers jersey, but to the young athlete, the cheer had a deeper meaning. It was to remind A. C. Green and his friends from church that they were striving to be champions for Christ.

At the age of seventeen, A.C. became a Christian and dedicated his life to the Lord. He continued his spiritual journey while attending Oregon State University. "In college, even though I had 7:30 a.m. lectures and labs some mornings, I made it a practice to get up by 6:00 a.m. to spend time with God."[1] This habit of spending time with God would continue throughout college, the sixteen years he played in the NBA, and today. He says, "The Bible is my manual for living.

> There are only two ways to live your life. One is as though nothing is a miracle. The other is as though everything is a miracle.
>
> —Albert Einstein

I have developed the habit of spending time with God and reading the Bible every morning."[2]

Now retired from the NBA, A.C. still holds the NBA Iron Man title for having played in 1,192 straight games. But most players and coaches remember him for another number—zero. That's the number of women he slept with as a professional basketball player.

"I made the decision as a teenager to be abstinent. I wanted to take control of my future. It wasn't a popular decision then, just like it can be an unpopular decision now."[3] When he started playing with the Lakers, A.C.'s convictions were known, but not yet proven. "A few players taunted, teased, tempted, and tried me to see if I'd hold up to my standards to save sex for marriage. 'You won't last two months in the NBA,' one of the guys told me."[4] But as they watched A.C. abstain in the face of temptation, the other players began to understand his faith and commitment weren't going to be shaken by their jeers. Eventually they got tired of trying to trip him up and left him alone.

A.C. wasn't entirely alone, though. His friends and church family encouraged his spiritual growth and stand. "The friends I have are true friends. True to themselves and true to me. We know each other's goals and dreams, and we encourage each other to achieve them."[5]

At midnight I will rise to give thanks to You, because of Your righteous judgments.
—Psalm 119:62

By making a commitment, growing in his relationship with Christ, and looking to his Christian friends to keep him accountable (he had a roommate the first four years he played in the NBA), A.C. Green was able to remain a virgin until he married the woman of his dreams—the year after he retired from professional basketball.

WHY KNOW IT?

✦ 32 percent of Protestant teenagers read the Bible, outside of church, weekly.[6]

✦ The younger a person is, the less likely he or she is to have a quiet time.[7]

✦ The average teen watches approximately 23 hours of television per week.[8]

✦ The average person will spend five years waiting in line, two years trying to return phone calls to people who aren't there, one year searching for misplaced items, six months sitting at red lights, and eight months opening junk mail.[9]

transfuse (trans FYOOZ): to cause to pass from one to another; transmit

For a very brief moment, *Quiet Riot* was a rock-and-roll phenomenon. Their name is a great description of our world, and their short-lived fame is prophetic of the amount of time most students can be still. The reason that the spiritual power of many students is waning is because this generation has a difficulty with the word *quiet*. We run everywhere, anytime—to the mall, to the Internet, to our cell phone—and we are restless in spirit. As a result, we don't understand our purpose and aren't able to stand strong.

> *Your word I have hidden in my heart, that I might not sin against You!*
> —Psalm 119:11

Then this Daniel distinguished himself above the governors and satraps, because an excellent spirit was in him; and the king gave thought to setting him over the whole realm. So the governors and satraps sought to find some charge against Daniel concerning the kingdom; but they could find no charge or fault, because he was faithful; nor was there any error or fault found in him. Then these men said, "We shall not find any charge against this Daniel unless we find it against him concerning the law of his God."

All . . . have consulted together to establish a royal statute and to make a firm decree, that whoever petitions any god or man for thirty days, except you, O king, shall be cast into the den of lions. Now when Daniel knew that the writing was signed, he went home. And in his upper room, with his windows open toward Jerusalem, he knelt down on his knees three times that day, and prayed and gave thanks before his God, as was his custom since early days. **—Daniel 6:3–5, 7, 10**

> **I have inclined my heart to perform Your statutes forever, to the very end.**
> —Psalm 119:112

In Daniel's time, Babylon was one of the most splendid cities of the ancient world. The state religion of Babylon involved big temples filled with large cults worshiping the great gods of the cities, who were ranked in an order corresponding to the political status of their cities. The multitude of cities and pantheons in Babylonia and the fluctuating political fortunes of the various cities throughout Babylonian history resulted in a great deal of conflict and confusion among the numerous cults.[10]

Young Daniel found himself working and living in Babylon after being kidnapped at the king's request. Far from home and in a different culture, he was in the minority. What's a young guy to do in that situation?

+ Daniel purposed in his heart that he would not defile himself.

+ Daniel kept the traditions of prayer, quiet time, and living a holy life.

+ Daniel focused on the Lord and left the world behind.

infuse (in FYOOZ)' to cause to be permeated with something (as a principle or quality) that alters usually for the better

AN EXCELLENT SPIRIT

First, Scripture tells us that Daniel had "an excellent spirit in him" (v. 3).

How would you like to be defined as *excellent in spirit?* This characteristic defined Daniel's daily routine, his personality, and his morals. Daniel was superior in both his attitude and ability. Notice that the emphasis is on the *spirit*, not the mind or body.

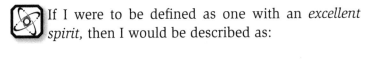 If I were to be defined as one with an *excellent spirit,* then I would be described as:

_____

_____

_____

Daniel didn't live for God because he was a geek; in fact, we know from Scripture that he was good-looking, talented, and intelligent. Daniel 1:4 describes Daniel and his friends as "young men in whom there was no blemish, but good-looking, gifted in all wisdom, possessing knowledge and quick to understand, who had ability to serve in the king's palace." These guys could have used personality and looks to take shortcuts, get favors, and be popular. Instead, they focused it all on habit. They chose to live a holy life.

Private Victories Precede Public Victories

Because Daniel was totally and wholeheartedly sold out to the Lord, those who were jealous of him said, "We won't find any way to get him unless it is about his God." What an incredible reputation!

The habit of kneeling to pray three times a day changed Daniel from the inside out. His private world gave him the strength and tenacity to live out a consistent public life.

 What or who is keeping me from this powerful, personal time with God?

A lot of people talk about the importance of a quiet time, but not many of them tell you how to do it. You might be wondering, "What am I supposed to do during my quiet time anyway?"

+ **Honor God**. Something amazing happens when you drop to your knees and come humbly and quietly before our majestic Lord. Immediately, when you bow the knee, you will find your heart ready to receive and to give love. Try it and see.

 When I humble myself before God, I am ready to serve man.

+ **Get into the Word.** Billy Graham once said that he reads five psalms for praise and worship every day and one chapter in Proverbs for wisdom. This gives him the ability to be rightly related to God and the wisdom to live skillfully with other people in daily and difficult situations. This program allows him to repeat the cycle once a month. You don't have to read whole chapters at a time; you can choose sections of Psalms or one or two verses in Proverbs. The point is to *read it and read it often.*

✦ **Quote the Scripture.** Say it often; say it loud. Keep Bible verses written on cards to take with you in the car or anyplace you might have wait time. When you say the Word out loud, you see it and hear it. When you write it, you have a triple advantage to making it your own. The Word of God is alive and has the power to change lives, get you through any trouble, and lead and guide you.

✦ **Journal your thoughts.** Write out the verse, and then think about what it says. Journal thoughts about:

✦ What changes need to be made in your life, what encouragement is there for you, and what instruction does the verse have for you?

✦ What does this verse say about serving others, how to love them, view them, and pray for them?

> *With my lips I have declared all the judgments of Your mouth.*
> —Psalm 119:13

✦ What does this verse say about God (He is truth, love, judge, mercy, compassion, power, etc.)?

_____

_____

_____

✦ Write one or more sentences of praise and thanksgiving based on the verse.

_____

_____

_____

✦ **Meditate on the Word.** Continue to think about the verse's meaning and how it applies to you throughout the day. When temptations or unwanted thoughts try to come in your mind, pop in the scripture and meditate on its power and meaning for your life. When you need to make a decision, think about the verse you are meditating on this week. This will put you in the habit of asking, "What would Jesus do in this situation?"

✦ **Memorize it.** There is no greater power to stay on the road to whom God has called you to be, or to gain victory in the moment of struggle, than knowing the Word of God. This is not the same as meditating. It is making a decided effort to write daily Scripture cards and carry them with you always.

✦ **Pray.** If you are having trouble saying meaningful prayers to God, try writing them out instead. To pray is literally "to think about" so that you can write it, say it, and think it all through the day. He wants to have a relationship with you in an intimate, genuine way. Use your daily scripture in a prayer by inserting your name or the name of someone you care about. For example, "Lord, help me to . . ."

✦ **Give God thanks.** There is great power in rehearsing what God has already done. There are so many things to be grateful for—such as your family, salvation, health, friends, and church. Thank God for His Word and who He is. When you put gratitude in your attitude, your heart is encouraged.

> *I will meditate on Your precepts, and contemplate Your ways.*
> —Psalm 119:15

✦ **Resolve to live the Word.** Make a decision to live out a part of the Word that you have read today. Whatever you read in your quiet time is what you want to purpose to do today. When you think about your day and what you want to accomplish, begin with what you have read, and think about how you can be a living Scripture during the day.

Select one of the scriptures used in today's lesson as your key focus this week. What is ONE THING that the verse instructs you to live out this week?

_____

_____

_____

Plan what, why, when, and how:

_____

_____

_____

When is the best time to have your quiet time? You can have a quiet time anytime you can sit still and *be quiet!* The morning is always the best time because you can begin your day with peace and strength. But you can take a brief moment in the morning, add to it in the afternoon, and finish up with time in the evening. It's your call.

Schedule your appointment with God, and purpose in your heart that no one and nothing will interfere. If a friend calls, say, "I'm tied up right now, but I'll call you back in about thirty minutes." If you get an IM, don't return it. In fact, shut off your phone, cell phone, and computer, and expect a supernatural time with the living God, Creator of the universe. Your friends will still be there when you are ready.

Believe it or not, God is waiting to hear from you!

diffuse (di FYOOZ) : to pour out and permit or cause to spread freely; to extend, scatter

When you think of Daniel, you may think automatically of how God delivered him in the lion's den and then promoted him in the kingdom of Babylon. But what you must first understand is how he became a man whom God blessed with a unique life.

Daniel became the kind of man God blessed through keeping the traditions of prayer and being true to God's Word. Hebrews 11:33 speaks of Daniel's kind of strong, personal faith that "subdued kingdoms, worked righteousness, obtained promises, stopped the mouths of lions." This type of faith cannot happen through a "Someday I will, I should have, I meant to" devotional life.

How can you build your personal faith this week? (Hint: Romans 10:17 says, "Faith comes by hearing and hearing by the Word of God.")

_____

_____

_____

GROUP DISCUSSION

Think of a situation you might face in the next few weeks in which you will be tested to stand for your faith—perhaps it is about a worldview issue such as evolution or abortion, or a discussion on moral purity. How can your quiet time prepare you for these situations? List three ways:

1. _____

2. _____

3. _____

Scripture reveals that Daniel had godly friends. In the midst of great persecution and discouragement, these guys stuck together and came out stronger. When we take the time to develop a genuine relationship with God, we are able to lead, influence, and encourage others.

[FUSE BOX]

An important step to a life of significance is to be known in your school and in your circle as a young man or woman of prayer for others, of quiet times with God, as a student who knows firsthand what he or she believes.

NOTES

> *Watch, stand fast in the faith, be brave, be strong.*
> —1 Corinthians 16:13

PRIVATE WORLD DEVOTIONS

MONDAY: See it. Read the surrounding passages or chapter for the Key Scripture so that you can get an understanding of the background and context. This helps you to really *see* the verse.

TUESDAY: Hear it. Read the daily Key Scripture and/or surrounding passage out loud, putting your name in, if applicable. For example, John *can do all things through Christ. Thieves have come to destroy* John, *but Jesus has come that* John *might have eternal life.*

WEDNESDAY: Write it. Write the verse and then what it says about:

✦ *Others:* Respond, serve, and love as Jesus would.

✦ *Me:* Specific attitudes, choices, or habits.

✦ *God:* His love, mercy, holiness, peace, joy, etc.

PRIVATE WORLD JOURNAL

I am grateful for—I praise you for—I am feeling—I am thinking—I need help with

PRIVATE WORLD DEVOTIONS *(Continued)*

THURSDAY: Memorize it. Take the verse with you—write it on a card or put it in your phone, iPod, or PDA. Go over it throughout the day so that it begins to *live* in your heart and mind.

FRIDAY: Pray it. Personalize the verse as you pray for yourself or for others or in praise to God. To pray is literally "to think about." Try thinking out loud or writing in your **PRIVATE WORLD JOURNAL.**

SATURDAY: Share it. Ask the Lord to bring someone to mind or in your path today who needs good news. Don't be shy—just let it out! Whether you IM, write, text, tell, or send it, the joy of God's Word will flow from your heart into theirs.

PRAYER REQUESTS

Date	Name	Need	Answer

PRIVATE WORLD JOURNAL

I am grateful for—I praise you for—I am feeling—I am thinking—I need help with

NOTES

CHAPTER 2

LIVE A LIFE OF WORSHIP

DAVID

KEY SCRIPTURE

I will bless the LORD at all times;
His praise shall continually be in my mouth.
My soul shall make its boast in the LORD;
The humble shall hear of it and be glad.

—Psalm 34:1–2

COULD THIS BE YOU?

Mac and Mark met while playing in the high school band. Mark was also in a rock band, and he asked Mac to join after hearing him sing at a senior assembly. Mac hung with the band for a while, but then he decided that he wanted to write and sing songs about his faith. Mark had another idea: "Why don't we start a Christian band?"[1] And the group that would later be known as Third Day began to take shape.

Worship: to honor or reverence; to regard with great or extravagant respect, honor, or devotion

David and Tai, who played for their youth group's band, joined the other two guys after Mark and Mac preformed at their church. A few years later, the band would be completed by Brad, who met the guys at a benefit concert. "We were Christians, and we wanted to glorify God with our music," says David.[2]

The band has sold millions of albums, won a Grammy, and received twenty-one Dove Awards,[3] but the guys didn't start out with money or fame in mind. "We wanted to start the band in the first place because we were excited about our faith," says Mark.[4] Throughout their success, the guys in Third Day have stayed focused. "We're Christians before we're musicians," Tai insists. "We love doing music. But if you took music away, I believe every guy in this band would find another way to serve God."[5] Brad adds, "Worship is bringing God to the center of whatever you're doing. It's not just about praise songs. You can worship God while walking down the street. You can worship God while washing dishes or at your job."[6]

WHY KNOW IT?

✦ 34 percent of teenagers like to spend their evenings hanging out with friends or family.[7]

✦ After school and before dinner, if students aren't busy with homework, they are most likely playing sports, watching TV, or hanging out with friends.[8]

✦ 25 percent of students participate in extracurricular activities—such as sports, music practice, or drama practice—after school.[9]

transfuse (trans FYOOZ): to cause to pass from one to another; transmit

All of us want to feel as though our life matters, that what we do is important and helpful to others. In the routine called life, it can feel like day after day goes by without real meaning or significance. We feel bored, restless, and uninspired.

David gives us a great example of a teen who had a boring job but managed to find adventure, inspiration, and courage through it. We find that his power came from within, and what set him apart from all the other young shepherd boys was a passion for seeking the Lord, a heart full of gratitude, and a quiet spirit of worship.

David said to Saul, "Your servant used to keep his father's sheep, and when a lion or a bear came and took a lamb out of the flock, I went out after it and struck it, and delivered the lamb from its mouth; and when it arose against me, I caught it by its beard, and struck and killed it. Your servant has killed both lion and bear; and this uncircumcised Philistine will be like one of them, seeing he has defied the armies of the living God." Moreover David said, "The Lord, who delivered me from the paw of the lion and from the paw of the bear, He will deliver me from the hand of this Philistine." And Saul said to David, "Go, and the Lord be with you!" —**1 Samuel 17:34–37**

Most of the time we think of David as the young guy who killed Goliath. It's true he was an incredible warrior, but David was not shy about where his strength came from. He was proud to tell Saul that he killed the lion and the bear, and he knew that his courage and skill came from the Lord.

infuse (in FYOOZ)**:** to cause to be permeated with something (as a principle or quality) that alters usually for the better

Let's look deeper at the life of David. What was it that allowed this young man to step up to fight the giant when no other adults dared to? Where did his courage come from?

The Power of Worship

David wrote the book of Psalms, and it is here that we see his true heart. He was a worshiper. If you are going to change the world, if you are going to do something for God, then you, too, must be a worshiper of the one and only true God. *When you worship, the presence of God comes and joins you in all that you do, and, together, you change the world.*

 How will my life change if I focus less on outward habits and more on inward worship?

The Power of Intentional Living

David grew up taking care of his father's sheep. He was in the fields most days and probably many nights. Taking care of sheep sounds like a boring job, but David made the most of it.

He made good use of his free time. David wasn't at the next flock over checking out the shepherdesses. He wasn't playing games by the well. He was becoming an extraordinary man of God. In his free time, David learned to play the harp. He wrote original songs. He watched the glory of creation alone in quiet, and the worship songs flowed from his heart.

What is ONE THING you could change about your free time? Select one thing that could change, and write the substitution for it.

What do you do with your free time?

When will you do this?

What do you need to do it successfully?

Who do you need help from?

How will you begin?

_____

_____

_____

✦ **He was alone with God, and the result was genuine worship**. In other words, the presence of God came into his life. David and God met one on one, and it was the power of this personal worship that made David who he became. *If you want to live a life of significance, then you need to have the heart of a worshiper.*

David escaped from these kings, and the result is a great psalm of praise to God and encouragement to others. Genuine worship moves us to tell others about the great, faithful, loving, good God.

diffuse (di FYOOZ); to pour out and permit or cause to spread freely; to extend, scatter

I will bless the LORD at all times; His praise shall continually be in my mouth. My soul shall make its boast in the Lord; The humble shall hear of it and be glad. Oh, magnify the LORD with me, And let us exalt His name together.
I sought the LORD, and He heard me, and delivered me from all my fears. They looked to Him and were radiant, and their faces were not ashamed. This poor man cried out, and the LORD heard him, and saved him out of all his troubles. The angel of the LORD encamps all around those who fear Him, and delivers them. Oh, taste and see that the LORD is good; Blessed is the man who trusts in Him! **—Psalm 34:1–8**

David gave us very intimate insights into his writings of praise. The psalms he wrote are beautiful and powerful and encouraging. Psalm 34 is one that David wrote during a difficult time in his life. He was forced to run from Saul, who wanted to kill him—only to find himself right in front of another king, Abimelech, who looked at him as a spy.

David escaped from these kings, and the result is a great psalm of praise to God and encouragement to others. *Genuine worship moves us to tell others about the great, faithful, loving, good God.*

In Psalm 34, we learn five things we need to do to have a life of significance:

1. Resolve to praise God at all times.

2. Point others to our source of joy.

3. Invite others to join in the worship.

4. Tell our unique story.

5. Proclaim the goodness of God.

Resolve to Praise God at All Times

David says, "I will bless the Lord at all times" (v. 1). David is quick here to pronounce to God and man that he has resolved in his heart to live by praise. Even when his circumstances were bad (like being chased by two kings who wanted to kill him), if no one else praised God, David made a decision and proclaimed it publicly: "I will praise God at all times."

GROUP DISCUSSION

What keeps you from worshiping God in your private world? Have you made any progress since last week's lesson?

_____

_____

_____

Do I spend more time thinking about what I can accomplish or on what God has already done?

Define what it means to have a life of significance:

_____

_____

_____

Point Others to Our Source of Joy

So that no one should give David praise, he directed them to the source of his joy. In Psalm 34:2, he said, "My soul shall make its boast in the LORD."

When the opportunity arises to stand up and defend the name of God, will you be ready? Will your inner power be enough to cause you to act outwardly in strength and courage?

_____

_____

How can you get ready?

_____

_____

_____

📖 Invite Others to Join in the Worship

David brings everyone in because this joy is too good to keep to himself. He says, "Magnify the LORD with me!" (v. 3).

Tell Our Unique Story

David begins to tell his story. Have you begun journaling your story? The ups and downs, ins and outs, the disappointments and the joys and how God ministered to you during each of these? These writings are not only great encouragement to you, but also to others. They provide a unique time of genuine worship with the one true God. Be sure to use the devotional journals included in this book.

📖 If you were to write a short psalm, what are some of the phrases you might use? Look at David's psalms as a guide.

_____

_____

_____

_____

_____

GROUP DISCUSSION

Write a short psalm of praise together by letting everyone contribute a phrase.

Proclaim the Goodness of God

David invites others to experience for themselves the goodness of God: "Oh, taste and see that the LORD is good!" (v. 8). How could you do anything but join in such a sincere zest for life?

 David wrote of his personal worship, and he told others about it. Be sure that you have such a vital, growing worship life that you can tell others about.

FUSE BOX

When you worship, the presence of God comes and joins you in all that you do, and, together, you change the world.

NOTES

Inner power drives
the outer actions.

PRIVATE WORLD DEVOTIONS

MONDAY: See it. Read the surrounding passages or chapter for the Key Scripture so that you can get an understanding of the background and context. This helps you to really *see* the verse.

TUESDAY: Hear it. Read the daily Key Scripture and/or surrounding passage out loud, putting your name in, if applicable. For example, <u>John</u> *can do all things through Christ. Thieves have come to destroy* <u>John</u>, *but Jesus has come that* <u>John</u> *might have eternal life.*

WEDNESDAY: Write it. Write the verse and then what it says about:

✦ *Others:* Respond, serve, and love as Jesus would.

✦ *Me:* Specific attitudes, choices, or habits.

✦ *God:* His love, mercy, holiness, peace, joy, etc.

PRIVATE WORLD JOURNAL

I am grateful for—I praise you for—I am feeling—I am thinking—I need help with

PRIVATE WORLD DEVOTIONS *(Continued)*

THURSDAY: Memorize it. Take the verse with you—write it on a card or put it in your phone, iPod, or PDA. Go over it throughout the day so that it begins to *live* in your heart and mind.

FRIDAY: Pray it. Personalize the verse as you pray for yourself or for others or in praise to God. To pray is literally "to think about." Try thinking out loud or writing in your **PRIVATE WORLD JOURNAL.**

SATURDAY: Share it. Ask the Lord to bring someone to mind or in your path today who needs good news. Don't be shy—just let it out! Whether you IM, write, text, tell, or send it, the joy of God's Word will flow from your heart into theirs.

PRAYER REQUESTS

Date	Name	Need	Answer

PRIVATE WORLD JOURNAL

I am grateful for—I praise you for—I am feeling—I am thinking—I need help with

NOTES

CHAPTER 3

PARTNER WITH OTHERS IN THE GOSPEL
TIMOTHY

KEY SCRIPTURE

No longer do I call you servants, for a servant does not know what his master is doing; but I have called you friends, for all things that I heard from My Father I have made known to you.

—John 15:15

COULD THIS BE YOU?

Hannah Luce is an American student who participates in short-term mission trips with Teen Mania Ministries. In her personal journal, she recorded the following about her latest experience:

> I am in Hydrabad, India, and we are seeing that more and more people here have no idea the bondage that has blinded their eyes. As my team and I pass through small villages, it breaks our hearts to think that for the first time even the older crowd is hearing about the name of Jesus and being set free from the chains of fear and pain. How can I stay silent and in the comforts of my own surroundings when here people would give their life for the sake of showing a single person the *Jesus* film? The faith that these people have in the billions of fake idols puts my personal faith in Jesus to shame. Knowing all these things, I have a responsibility to live a life of a world changer despite my age or surroundings. I

will live a life of faith, and no matter what the cost: I just want to change the world.

WHY KNOW IT?

✦ America is one of the largest mission fields in the world, and the American church is the most richly endowed body of believers on the planet.[1]

✦ 2 million teenagers go on short-term mission trips each year.[2]

✦ As Christianity has spread to other countries by American mission efforts, it has simultaneously declined in America.[3]

transfuse (trans FYOOZ)', to cause to pass from one to another; transmit

Timothy grew up hearing about the things of God. His mother and grandmother probably took him to the synagogue every Sabbath, and he grew into spiritual independence as a great young man of God. His Greek father may have died when Timothy was young, because only his mother and grandmother are mentioned in the Scriptures as being devout in the faith and passing on this heritage to him.

And my God shall supply all your need according to His riches in glory by Christ Jesus.
—Philippians 4:19

Deeply impressed by the apostle Paul's preaching and ministry, Timothy was well grounded. The stoning and beatings Paul endured did not frighten him. In Acts 16, Timothy is called "a disciple" who was "well spoken of" by those in the church (vv. 1–2). His reputation preceded him as a young man Paul could depend on.

Students often look for opportunities to travel the country or go overseas, but Timothy shows us that the labor must begin at home. One ancient proverb says, "The light that shines the farthest shines the brightest at home."

Paul, an apostle of Jesus Christ by the will of God, according to the promise of life which is in Christ Jesus, to Timothy, a beloved son: Grace, mercy, and peace from God the Father and Christ Jesus our Lord. I thank God, whom I serve with a pure conscience, as my forefathers did, as without ceasing I remember you in my prayers night and day, greatly desiring to see you, being mindful of your tears, that I may be filled with joy, when I call to remembrance the genuine faith that is in you, which dwelt first in your grandmother Lois and your mother Eunice, and I am persuaded is in you also. Therefore I remind you to stir up the gift of God which is in you through the laying on of my hands. For God has not given us a spirit of fear, but of power and of love and of a sound mind. —**2 Timothy 1:1–7**

Timothy must have been shy, because Paul assured him that "God has not given us a spirit of fear" (v. 7). If anyone ever had a reason to be fearful, it would be Timothy. Naturally shy, the responsibilities of the apostle Paul were now being placed on his young shoulders. As Timothy is faced with perils and difficulties, Paul writes to him personally to encourage his faith.

infuse (in FYOOZ) ; to cause to be permeated with something (as a principle or quality) that alters usually for the better

A Significant Life Is Accountable

When you read through the book of Acts, you find neither Paul nor Timothy traveled alone. If these men, used of God and powerful in anointing, needed partners in the gospel, how can we even begin to think we can do it alone?

An accountability friendship is not a casual suggestion; it is an absolute imperative.

+ An accountability partner cancels out the opportunity to cover up emotional problems, sin, or temptation, and to pretend all is OK when it's not.

+ Accountability partners give permission to get in one another's faces. They don't just say, "I'm praying for you." They ask, "What are you doing about your quiet time? How are you handling temptation?"

+ Accountability partners remind you that life is not about getting by; it's about living with influence and purpose. They remind you of God's call on your life and what you have to do to get there.

+ An accountability friendship is an intimate friendship. In order for your friends to really pray for you, they need to know your deepest fears and your highest dreams. You can sing in church next to someone for a year, share goose bumps and tears, but never help each other live with victory and strength.

Your accountability partners should be people with whom you are committed to sharing your heart, the very deepest part of yourself. This was the kind of friendship Jesus had with His disciples as described in John 15:15: "No longer do I call you servants, for a servant does not know what his master is doing; but I have called you friends, for all things that I heard from My Father I have made known to you."

> *So [Paul] sent into Macedonia two of those who ministered to him, Timothy and Erastus, but he himself stayed in Asia for a time.*
> —Acts 19:22

These are the kind of relationships that Timothy and Paul had, and these two had a part in changing the world, just as you want to do.

Pray about a person (of the same gender) who could be a strong accountability partner with you, and ask God to help you meet and arrange this relationship.

What time could you meet each week?

_____

_____

_____

Could you also partner together with other friends through phone or e-mail?

_____

_____

_____

Consider making your parents part of your accountability team. Doing this shows your absolute commitment to their authority and your willingness to be completely honest. This honors and pleases God and gives you the opportunity to live a consistent life without secrets or regrets.

A Significant Life Is One That Serves Others

Paul sent two of his helpers, one of whom was Timothy, to Macedonia to minister in his place. Timothy, who had walked alongside Paul as a young man carrying the scrolls, luggage, and running errands, was now sent to lead and teach on behalf of Paul. Timothy probably began with errands and administrative duties, but in the books of 2 Corinthians, Philippians, Colossians, 1 and 2 Thessalonians, and Philemon, we see that Timothy was given a more active role. As Paul told the Corinthians, "I have sent Timothy to you, who is my beloved and faithful son in the Lord, who will remind you of my ways in Christ, as I teach everywhere in every church" (1 Corinthians 4:17).

The word *bondservant* is from the Greek *to bind.*

Timothy showed himself trustworthy through a servant-hearted friendship to Paul, and Paul in turned trusted Timothy to serve alongside him in Christian history.

Are the plans I have for my free time, particularly for my summer, plans that will allow me to serve others and to share the good news?

What steps can I take to become a partner in an effective existing ministry?

1. _____

2. _____

3. _____

What habits do I need to establish to become a servant leader as Timothy did?

Timothy started by carrying Paul's scrolls and running errands for him. Don't hesitate to begin with the small things!

When Paul wrote to the church at Philippi, he addressed the letter from "Paul and Timothy, bondservants of Jesus Christ" (Philippians 1:1). Timothy went from suitcase carrier to assistant scribe, teacher, and leader.

With all of Timothy's honors came a new title: Paul calls himself and Timothy "bondservants of Jesus Christ." *Bondservant* was not a flattering term in their society, for this was the lowest of classes; but to these Christians, it was a privileged title.

> If the apostle Paul needed an accountability partner, how much more will we need one?

+ A *bondservant* is a person bound to another in slavery by birth. Paul wants the church to know that he has been born again into a spiritual bondage to serve Christ, which he holds as a privilege and a joy.

+ The union between bondservant and master could only be broken through death; it was permanent, just as we are joined to Christ for eternity.

+ *Bondservant* refers to one whose will is swallowed up in the will of another. Paul and Timothy yielded themselves to the will of God in all things.[4]

diffuse (di FYOOZ) : to pour out and permit or cause to spread freely; to extend, scatter

Paul and Timothy delighted in being bondservants for their Lord.

A Significant Life Is Mission-Minded

Timothy left behind his home and family to travel the world with Paul—and later, he continued to travel the world without him. World missions permeated and drove Timothy's life.

How do you become mission-minded?

Disciple: one whose life is marked by discipline and the willingness to learn.

◆ **Pray.** Pray for missionaries by name in other countries, for remote areas, for those your church supports. Pray until you feel God's broken heart for those who are far from Him. Pray until you weep with the compassion of God rising up in your heart. Pray that God will raise up people to reach the unreached people groups. This should be a part of your regular quiet time.

Consider starting and leading a prayer group that focuses on praying for missionaries in a particular foreign country.

Do ONE THING to take you toward that goal this week. Commit today to:

◆ Research missionaries who are asking for prayer.

OR

◆ Ask godly friends to commit to a specific prayer time.

> **Missions is when you use your life to change somebody else's.**

Who can you ask? Write their names below, and then ask them!

1. _____

2. _____

3. _____

◆ **Go!** Commit to go yourself. Jesus said, "The harvest truly is great, but the laborers are few; therefore pray the Lord of the harvest to send out laborers into His harvest. Go your way; behold, I send you out as lambs among wolves" (Luke 10:2–3). In verse 2, the Lord tells the disciples to pray for missionary laborers; but in the very next sentence, He tells them, "Go." This command indicates a change of location. It implies getting up from the routine and going to a new place.

Stay faithful to the call of God to "go" and reach the lost. Don't fall for the lie that says "everyone worships the same god by a different name."

Don't worry about the money. There may be a lot of reasons that you feel you can't go on a mission trip—lack of funds, lack of knowledge, or young age—but none of these are valid when you consider God's command to "go." Make the commitment, start to save and earn money, and pray, "Here I am, Lord; send me." Do you think that God cannot supply enough money for you to go and minister to one whom He loves? Be prepared to sacrifice a hamburger, movie, CD, iPod download, or other extras in your life in favor of a much richer reward.

Consider planning an annual mission trip as a tradition that you begin as a student and will carry over into your adulthood.

GROUP DISCUSSION

What are some money-wasting habits and/or non-essential purchases that you can set aside? List two:

1. _____

2. _____

How much money do you think you could realistically save in one year if you changed just two spending habits?

_____

_____

FUSE BOX

Dare to believe that God will use you to change the lives of others by making plans this week to go on a mission trip. God will supply; He will make a way. Contact the missions committee at your local church or go to www.globalexpeditions.com for more information.

PRIVATE WORLD DEVOTIONS

MONDAY: See it. Read the surrounding passages or chapter for the Key Scripture so that you can get an understanding of the background and context. This helps you to really *see* the verse.

TUESDAY: Hear it. Read the daily Key Scripture and/or surrounding passage out loud, putting your name in, if applicable. For example, <u>John</u> *can do all things through Christ. Thieves have come to destroy* <u>John</u>, *but Jesus has come that* <u>John</u> *might have eternal life.*

WEDNESDAY: Write it. Write the verse and then what it says about:

+ *Others:* Respond, serve, and love as Jesus would.

+ *Me:* Specific attitudes, choices, or habits.

+ *God:* His love, mercy, holiness, peace, joy, etc.

PRIVATE WORLD JOURNAL

I am grateful for—I praise you for—I am feeling—I am thinking—I need help with

PRIVATE WORLD DEVOTIONS *(Continued)*

THURSDAY: Memorize it. Take the verse with you—write it on a card or put it in your phone, iPod, or PDA. Go over it throughout the day so that it begins to *live* in your heart and mind.

FRIDAY: Pray it. Personalize the verse as you pray for yourself or for others or in praise to God. To pray is literally "to think about." Try thinking out loud or writing in your **PRIVATE WORLD JOURNAL.**

SATURDAY: Share it. Ask the Lord to bring someone to mind or in your path today who needs good news. Don't be shy—just let it out! Whether you IM, write, text, tell, or send it, the joy of God's Word will flow from your heart into theirs.

PRAYER REQUESTS

Date	Name	Need	Answer

PRIVATE WORLD JOURNAL

I am grateful for—I praise you for—I am feeling—I am thinking—I need help with

NOTES

CHAPTER 4

MAKE NO COMPROMISE

SHADRACH, MESHACH, AND ABED-NEGO

KEY SCRIPTURE

And I give them eternal life, and they shall never perish; neither shall anyone snatch them out of My hand. My Father, who has given them to Me, is greater than all; and no one is able to snatch them out of My Father's hand.

—**John 10:28–29**

COULD THIS BE YOU?

Chris King was going to Harvard, and the experience would prove to be a climate change from his home in Orlando, Florida, in more ways than one. "Growing up in Central Florida, I had been raised by a family who placed great importance on my spiritual life. I attended First Presbyterian Church of Orlando from the time I was a little boy, and I became active in the Fellowship of Christian Athletes in my high school years, frequently sharing my beliefs with groups of students."[1] But mentioning his desire to become involved in an on-campus ministry during a freshman orientation event got a strange reaction—silence. A few weeks later, a counselor who'd been at the event would tell him his comments were "brave."[2]

Chris decided to run for student body president. Chris and running mate Fentrice Driskell ran on a platform of "building a healthier

Harvard community."[3] Chris and Fentrice met with student groups about sharing vision and unity on campus. Their campaign seemed to be off to a good start, and it was a close race.

Then they received an unsolicited endorsement. A lady on the Undergraduate Council Election Commission asked her friends to pray for the candidates, "especially Team King-Driskell," whose message was "vital for Harvard's undergraduate program."[4] Word spread that Chris was a Christian. Soon, freshman dorms were covered with fliers about his "hidden Christian agenda" with untrue statements about his campaign. The campus newspaper published an editorial saying, "Their promise of 'values-driven leadership' is vague and worrisome; though King and running-mate Fentrice Driskell say they want to unify the campus, their ties to religious groups have raised concerns among many students."[5] The editorial concluded that Chris was unfit to be president because he was a Christian, and the paper endorsed another candidate.

The anti-Christian sentiment came as a surprise to Chris and to his opponent, Noah Seton. "The issue of religion became the surprise issue," said Seton. "King's platform certainly was not a platform you would associate with the Christian Right."[6] But Chris was labeled a bigot and a religious extremist because of his faith. He lost the election by one hundred votes. Seton's team indicated that they would have investigated the smear campaign if it had happened to them, but they also understood that Chris and Fentrice just wanted to put the whole thing behind them.

Chris went on to graduate from Harvard, and he said this about his experience: "As I processed toward graduation, the big moments of my life at Harvard raced across my mind. As they did, I felt a sense of triumph because unlike some of my friends who came to Harvard from all across America as Christians, I would also leave

> And I give them eternal life, and they shall never perish; neither shall anyone snatch them out of My hand. My Father, who has given them to Me, is greater than all; and no one is able to snatch them out of My Father's hand.
> —John 10:28–29

Harvard with my faith intact and strengthened by the challenges I faced."[7]

WHY KNOW IT?

✦ The Establishment Clause of the First Amendment does not prohibit purely private religious speech by students.

✦ "Students have the same right to engage in individual or group prayer and religious discussion during the school day as they do to engage in other comparable activity. For example, students may read their Bibles or other scriptures, say grace before meals, and pray before tests to the same extent they may engage in comparable nondisruptive activities."[8]

✦ "Students in informal settings, such as cafeterias and hallways, may pray and discuss their religious views with each other, subject to the same rules of order as apply to other student activities and speech. Students may also speak to, and attempt to persuade, their peers about religious topics just as they do with regard to political topics. School officials, however, should intercede to stop student speech that constitutes harassment aimed at a student or a group of students."[9]

✦ "Students may also participate in before or after school events with religious content on the same terms as they may participate in other noncurriculum activities on school premises. School officials may neither discourage nor encourage participation in such an event."[10]

✦ The Equal Access Act is designed to ensure that, consistent with the First Amendment, student religious activities are accorded the same access to public school facilities as are student secular activities.[11]

transfuse (trans FYOOZ) : to cause to pass from one
to another; transmit

The pressure to bend our convictions has come from the agenda of acceptance—that is, to accept lifestyles and attitudes that are less than the absolute truths found in the Word of God. Nowhere in the Word are we told to hate the sinner or not to be any less than loving toward those who do not believe as we do. Jesus gave us the superior example of walking through the crowd without *being* the crowd. You can love others without changing the message of who Christ is and what you believe.

Nebuchadnezzar the king made an image of gold, whose height was sixty cubits and its width six cubits. He set it up in the plain of Dura, in the province of Babylon. . . . Then a herald cried aloud: "To you it is commanded, O peoples, nations, and languages, that at the time you hear the sound of the horn, flute, harp, lyre, and psaltery, in symphony with all kinds of music, you shall fall down and worship the gold image that King Nebuchadnezzar has set up; and whoever does not fall down and worship shall be cast immediately into the midst of a burning fiery furnace." So at that time, when all the people heard the sound of the horn, flute, harp, and lyre, in symphony with all kinds of music, all the people, nations, and languages fell down and worshiped the gold image which King Nebuchadnezzar had set up. —**Daniel 3:1, 4–7**

In the country of Babylon, the norm was to worship a tall idol in the shape of Nebuchadnezzar, the king. This is the same country we know today as Iraq.

Throughout the years of his reign of terror, Saddam Hussein portrayed himself as the successor to Nebuchadnezzar. One biographer quoted him as saying, "Nebuchadnezzar stirs in me everything relating to pre-Islamic ancient history. And what is most important to me about Nebuchadnezzar is the link between the Arabs's abilities and the liberation of Palestine. Nebuchadnezzar was, after all, an Arab from Iraq, albeit ancient Iraq. That is why whenever I remember Nebuchadnezzar I like to remind the Arabs, Iraqis in particular, of their historical responsibilities. It is a burden that should . . . spur them into action because of their history."[12] The truth is that Nebuchadnezzar was neither Arab nor Muslim, but Saddam Hussein's "Nebuchadnezzar Imperial Complex," as one psychologist called it, has been remarkably consistent.

> To compromise your convictions is like the disease of leprosy. It starts with one or two small sores, but before long it consumes the entire body.

infuse (in FYOOZ) : to cause to be permeated with something (as a principle or quality) that alters usually for the better

The Pressure

In the days of these three young Hebrews, everyone was expected to worship Nebuchadnezzar. Can you say *ego*? This was way more than just peer pressure: notice that "all the people, nations, and languages" worshiped the image. This wasn't a suggestion; it was a law, one that was punishable and enforceable by death of the worst kind—that is, being burned alive.

Compare the three Hebrews's situation to the criticism you might get if you carry a Bible to school or don't participate in certain behaviors and parties. Really, there is no comparison. What we have today is simply an assault by people who have no inner purpose in an effort to make you feel inferior. If they can embarrass you or make you look unreasonable, then they are sure you will give in to the lifestyle of whatever seems right.

Wrestler Ted Dibiase used to play a villain in the wrestling world of what was the WWF, now called the WWE. Ted became famous for his Wrestlemania battles with Hulk Hogan and others. With his trademark evil laugh, he called himself "The Million Dollar Man." Ted used to say, "Every man can be bought. Every man has a price." His face was on lunch boxes, action figures, and video games, and he enjoyed celebrity status everywhere. But the truth, Ted will tell you, is that his life was empty, his relationships were broken, and he felt like life wasn't worth living.

Ted Dibiase found out the truth when his wife shared genuine salvation with him. He now travels the country telling students, "Everyone does have a price, but that price was paid by the Lord Jesus on the cross at Calvary, and none of us ever has to pay it again. Now that I have accepted Christ, I am no longer for sale." When Christ took away our obligation to punishment, He laid upon us a new obligation to obedience.

Open your right hand. Now imagine this is the hand of Christ and you are in the center. Close that hand, and then close the left hand around it. This is the Father's hand. No one and nothing can get to you unless they first go through the Father and then through the Son. The three young Hebrews believed that, and they were right.

The Accusers

There are certain Jews whom you have set over the affairs of the province of Babylon: Shadrach, Meshach, and Abed-Nego; these men, O king, have not paid due regard to you. They do not serve your gods or worship the gold image which you have set up." Then Nebuchadnezzar, in rage and fury, gave the command to bring Shadrach, Meshach, and Abed-Nego. —**Daniel 3:12–13**

In this case, these three friends were criticized for what they didn't do rather than what they did. They simply refused to worship anything or anyone other than their God. Their accusers were standing nearby, ready to turn them in.

Do you have accusers at school who watch you and want to trip you up because of what you don't do? Your best defense is a consistent life of purpose and passion for Christ. Be known as one who always chooses to do the right thing, regardless of opinion, pressure, or circumstance.

GROUP DISCUSSION

How important was the friendship of Shadrach, Meshach, and Abed-Nego? How much of an impact do you think they had on one another in this decision? If you have to stand against this type of accusation, do you have friends or accountability partners who can stand with you? Who?

diffuse (di FYOOZ) : to pour out and permit or cause to spread freely; to extend, scatter

The Intimidation

So they brought these men before the king. Nebuchadnezzar spoke, saying to them, "Is it true, Shadrach, Meshach, and Abed-Nego, that you do not serve my gods or worship the gold image which I have set up? Now if you are ready at the time you hear the sound of the horn, flute, harp, lyre, and psaltery, in symphony with all kinds of music, and you fall down and worship the image which I have made, good! But if you do not worship, you shall be cast immediately into the midst of a burning fiery furnace. And who is the god who will deliver you from my hands?" **—Daniel 3:13–15**

The three young men were brought before the king and given another chance. Nebuchadnezzar offered them a chance to escape the fiery furnace by compromising their faith. He said, "Now, if you are ready . . . fall down" (v. 15). Shadrach, Meshach, and Abed-Nego were indeed ready for the king's question, because they had prepared their hearts since childhood.

The Response

Shadrach, Meshach, and Abed-Nego answered and said to the king, "O Nebuchadnezzar, we have no need to answer you in this matter. If that is the case, our God whom we serve is able to deliver us from the burning fiery furnace, and He will deliver us from your hand, O king. But if not, let it be known to you, O king, that we do not serve your gods, nor will we worship the gold image which you have set up." **—Daniel 3:16–18**

Shadrach, Meschach, and Abed-Nego were made of steel. Can you imagine this scene? You would think that these three teens would be shaking, crying, and begging for their lives, but they let the king know that they would not persuade him either way because they trusted God for the final outcome. Their goal in this test was that God would be honored, and they were not willing to waver from that.

Think about a situation in your school in which you might be put on the spot for your faith. Would you be ready to stand if asked to compromise?

What is ONE THING you could be ready to share about your personal faith with someone else? (Have a Scripture and a personal story ready—the Lord could bring someone to you even this week!)

_____

_____

_____

_____

NO COMPROMISE:
Nothing about their answer was tentative because nothing in their heart was unsure.

Ready to stand means that you are:

✦ Active and strong in your faith;

✦ Sure in your understanding of Scripture;

✦ Surrounded by like-minded, godly friends.

Think about getting "ready to stand" this week. Establish habits in your life that will prepare you for a "no compromise" lifestyle.

Who or what are you intimidated by? What causes you to want to join the crowd rather than stand against it? What makes you feel inferior or embarrassed?

> Courageous
> faith doesn't come at
> the last minute. It is
> a lifelong habit.

What can you do to recognize and banish the intimidation?

The Protected Life

> *Then Nebuchadnezzar was full of fury, and the expression on his face changed toward Shadrach, Meshach, and Abed-Nego. He spoke and commanded that they heat the furnace seven times more than it was usually heated. And he commanded certain mighty men of valor who were in his army to bind Shadrach, Meshach, and Abed-Nego, and cast them into the burning fiery furnace. Then these men were bound in their coats, their trousers, their turbans, and their other*

garments, and were cast into the midst of the burning fiery furnace. Therefore, because the king's command was urgent, and the furnace exceedingly hot, the flame of the fire killed those men who took up Shadrach, Meshach, and Abed-Nego. And these three men, Shadrach, Meshach, and Abed-Nego, fell down bound into the midst of the burning fiery furnace.

*Then King Nebuchadnezzar was astonished; and he rose in haste and spoke, saying to his counselors, "Did we not cast three men bound into the midst of the fire?" They answered and said to the king, "True, O king." "Look!" he answered, "I see four men loose, walking in the midst of the fire; and they are not hurt, and the form of the fourth is like the Son of God." —***Daniel 3:19–25***

The identity of the fourth figure who appeared in the fire has been the subject of some discussion. Was it a preincarnate appearance of Jesus Christ, or was it an angel? Most would agree that it was a revelation of the protection of God.

God let Nebuchadnezzar know that He alone ultimately has the power over life and death. These three young men would not bend and would not bow to anyone else. They were, therefore, protected by God and could not burn.

What kind of consequence do you face by not compromising your faith? It's probably not being thrown into a fire! It's more like just a bit of criticism and teasing. Keep your backbone straight and your head up. When you walk with purpose, God is there to walk alongside you. And He's not a bad bodyguard!

If friendships are important to you, how important would they be to a person without Christ as he or she tries to find purpose and truth?

We need to let people know that God will be with them and protect them if they stand by their beliefs by faith.

How could you be that friend?

How do you think a godly friendship can help you stand against criticism and intimidation?

Good Publicity

And the satraps, administrators, governors, and the king's counselors gathered together, and they saw these men on whose bodies the fire had no power; the hair of their head was not singed nor were their garments affected, and the smell of fire was not on them. —**Daniel 3:27**

Not only were these three faithful young men not burned, but not even *the smell of fire* was on them! God rules and overrules! Their boldness to stand faithful to God's honor became not only a public discussion, but one for all of history. You are reading about it today, and your children will also read about it someday.

 Can you think of anything you can do that will influence history?

_____

_____

Start where you are—this week.

✦ Be consistent.

✦ Show yourself friendly to those who act unfriendly.

✦ Keep friends accountable to the Scripture.

✦ Share your faith.

FUSE BOX

Those who live for significance stand together in times of testing. Your closest friends must be as on fire for God as you are.

_____

_____

_____

PRIVATE WORLD DEVOTIONS

MONDAY: See it. Read the surrounding passages or chapter for the Key Scripture so that you can get an understanding of the background and context. This helps you to really *see* the verse.

TUESDAY: Hear it. Read the daily Key Scripture and/or surrounding passage out loud, putting your name in, if applicable. For example, <u>John</u> *can do all things through Christ. Thieves have come to destroy* <u>John</u>, *but Jesus has come that* <u>John</u> *might have eternal life.*

WEDNESDAY: Write it. Write the verse and then what it says about:

✦ *Others:* Respond, serve, and love as Jesus would.

✦ *Me:* Specific attitudes, choices, or habits.

✦ *God:* His love, mercy, holiness, peace, joy, etc.

PRIVATE WORLD JOURNAL

I am grateful for—I praise you for—I am feeling—I am thinking—I need help with

PRIVATE WORLD DEVOTIONS *(Continued)*

THURSDAY: Memorize it. Take the verse with you—write it on a card or put it in your phone, iPod, or PDA. Go over it throughout the day so that it begins to *live* in your heart and mind.

FRIDAY: Pray it. Personalize the verse as you pray for yourself or for others or in praise to God. To pray is literally "to think about." Try thinking out loud or writing in your **PRIVATE WORLD JOURNAL.**

SATURDAY: Share it. Ask the Lord to bring someone to mind or in your path today who needs good news. Don't be shy—just let it out! Whether you IM, write, text, tell, or send it, the joy of God's Word will flow from your heart into theirs.

PRAYER REQUESTS

Date	Name	Need	Answer

PRIVATE WORLD JOURNAL

I am grateful for—I praise you for—I am feeling—I am thinking—I need help with

NOTES

CHAPTER 5

KEEP AN OPEN HEART

LYDIA

KEY SCRIPTURE

That if you confess with your mouth the Lord Jesus and believe in your heart that God has raised Him from the dead, you will be saved. For with the heart one believes unto righteousness, and with the mouth confession is made unto salvation.

—Romans 10:9–10

COULD THIS BE YOU?

Jennifer, a self-proclaimed atheist, found it humorous that a Christian girl in her dorm would help her stumble up the stairs after she came in from a night of drinking.[1] "I was such a mess," Jennifer says. "I was battling alcoholism at the time, smoking four packs of cigarettes a day, and cussing like a sailor."[2] But Jennifer's rude remarks, mocking, and behavior weren't enough to discourage the girl in her dorm. "Day after day, despite what my attitude was or how mean I was to her, she just continued to show me the love of Christ and continued to speak the truth to me. She understood that a lot of things I was choosing to do, and a lot of the sins I was committing, reflected a lack of understanding of how much God

> Build your confidence upon this: "He who has begun a good work in you will complete it."
> —Philippians 1:6

loved me. Little by little, I started to realize that God really did love me and that the sacrifice Christ made was just something I needed so desperately."[3]

Two months later, the impact, influence, and friendship of the girl in her dorm led Jennifer to Christ. "I was just so amazed by God's forgiveness and God's grace that I would be on my knees at night praying and crying to God, 'Please, don't ever let me not believe in you.' I was so afraid 'cause other people were watching me change, going, 'Oh, this is just a fad; this isn't going to last. As soon as she realizes this is not real, she's gonna leave.' I just kept praying that wouldn't be the case."[4]

> It takes 20 years to build a reputation and five minutes to ruin it. If you think about that, you'll do things differently.
>
> —Warren Buffett

A classically trained musician, Jennifer was attending Pittsburg State University on a music scholarship.[5] She began expressing her awe of God through music, which she would share with others at local coffeehouses. In time, Jennifer Knapp would go on to win the Dove Award for Best New Artist, be called "a rising star" by the *L.A. Times*, be described by *People* magazine as "an uncommonly literate songwriter," and see more than 850,000 copies of her first two albums sold.[6]

After all her success and reaching millions of people, Jennifer still remains humble, stating, "It's amazing how the simple gospel message has so much power. Knowing that gives me courage to be vocal. It's not what I say—it's what Jesus says and does through me. Realizing salvation comes through Christ alone has made a huge impact on me."[7]

WHY KNOW IT?

+ 43 percent of Christians made their salvation decision by the age of 13, and 64 percent of Christians made their decision before turning 18.[8]

+ Among the 60 percent of teenagers who profess to be committed Christians, only half qualify as born-again Christians, a categorization that includes having "made a personal commitment to Jesus Christ that is still important in [their] life today."[9]

+ 83 percent of teenagers believe that moral truth depends on circumstances.[10]

+ Among teenagers professing to be Christians, only 9 percent say they believed in moral absolutes.[11]

+ The total number of new religious movements—including cults that are psychologically destructive—is estimated to be in the tens of thousands.[12]

transfuse (trans FYOOZ): to cause to pass from one to another; transmit

When you give your life to Christ, you come alive on the inside. Your spirit is made brand new, and you are born again. When you understand that "all have sinned and fall short of the glory of God" (Romans 3:23), then you understand that salvation is not about religion or "being good." When you try and base salvation on being good, you can always find someone who is "worse" than you, until you consider Jesus. He was sinless; therefore, salvation is the gift of God by grace and not of works.

*If you confess with your mouth the Lord
Jesus and believe in your heart that God
has raised Him from the dead, you will be
saved. For with the heart one believes unto
righteousness, and with the mouth confession
is made unto salvation.* —**Romans 10:9–10**

Romans 10:9–10 makes it clear how a person can receive
God's free gift of salvation. Simply call on the name of
Jesus, asking Him to forgive your sins and to come into
your heart. As you do, you are receiving the gift of eternal life.

infuse (in FYOOZ)ʼ: to cause to be permeated with something
(as a principle or quality) that alters usually for the better

The apostle Paul made his way across the known
world to preach the gospel as the Holy Spirit directed
him. He traveled by foot, by beast, by boat, and hitched
a ride any way he could. His ship sailed throughout
Macedonia, and he made his way to the various colonies, preaching and starting churches as he went. Sometimes he was well received and sometimes he was run
out of town.

A Heart Open to Genuine Salvation

*And on the Sabbath day we went out of
the city to the riverside, where prayer was
customarily made; and we sat down and spoke
to the women who met there.* —**Acts 16:13**

One particular trip took Paul to the foremost city of Macedonia, a colony called Philippi. Down at the riverside at
a prayer meeting, he met Lydia. "Now a certain woman

named Lydia heard us. She was a seller of purple from the city of Thyatira, who worshiped God" (Acts 16:14).

Lydia was at the riverside because she knew it was a place where prayer meetings were held. She was a woman who was devoted to religion but had no personal power or genuine faith. Lydia went to prayer meetings, talked about God, and was curious to know more. She tried very hard to read the Scripture and to pray, but no one had shown her the truth about salvation.

When Lydia heard Paul's message of genuine salvation, she suddenly realized that *knowing* **about** *God is not the same as* **knowing God.** Scripture says, "The Lord opened her heart to heed the things spoken by Paul" (Acts 16:14).

Jesus hung out with the disciples to encourage them—but also to be encouraged. Cultivate the habit of hanging out "by the riverside," where you know prayer meetings and those who love God will gather. This is a great place to bring those who know about God but do not know Him personally.

Have you come to the place in your life where you know for sure that if you died tonight, you would go to heaven? Do you *know* Christ, or do you only *know about* Him? Lydia opened her heart on a definite day and time at the river, and she was changed.

Do you remember specifically when you opened your heart to Christ and were changed?

If so, write a few sentences to describe it:

_____

_____

_____

_____

If you aren't sure, take a minute after class to speak with the class leader. Christ died for you because He loves you and is ready to forgive you and give eternal life: "For whoever calls on the name of the Lord shall be saved" (Romans 10:13).

A Heart Ready to Obey Christ

As a wealthy businesswoman, Lydia's friendship with these strangers called "Christians," and Paul in particular, was risky. But something touched her, and she opened her heart to understand this new teaching about Paul's God. "And when she and her household were baptized, she begged us, saying, 'If you have judged me to be faithful to the Lord, come to my house and stay.' So she persuaded us" (Acts 16:15).

The change in Lydia was immediate and genuine.

✦ She wanted to be identified as a Christian in baptism as a public declaration of a private decision.

✦ She wanted to be a servant and help others with the same faith she had just received.

We see that Lydia was not only open to the teaching, but she was obedient to the teaching. When the Holy Spirit came into her life, the result was both a changed private life and public life. Lydia was willing to risk opening her home to these travelers because she was willing to open her heart to faith.

Have you made a public profession of your private decision? If not, speak to a leader about this. It is an important part of courageous faith.

When you read God's Word, are you motivated to serve others? Do you follow through?

_____

_____

_____

diffuse (di FYOOZ), to pour out and permit or cause to spread freely; to extend, scatter

A Changed Heart

Inviting Paul and his friends to her home was only the beginning for Lydia. She wanted the city to know that she wasn't just a successful business-woman, but that she was a successful Christian busi-nesswoman. She opened her home to start a church, and the talk across the city went flying. She went public with showing *the grace of God.*

Against the current culture, Lydia's home church was one where:

✦ Jew and Greek sat together;

✦ slaves and masters worshiped side by side;

✦ men and women worshiped together.

Lydia was willing to be talked about for the sake of the gospel. As the saying goes, "Any publicity is good publicity!" Her church was known for its outrageous so-cial behavior, but Lydia described it as the grace of Christ available to everyone. While many cried, "It's an out-rage!" Lydia displayed a public life of worship. Her open, obedient heart was laced with tough resolve.

Think about Christian behavior that is contrary to your school such as a "no clique" policy or friendship with the unpopular. Are you willing to be talked about for the sake of the gospel?

What is ONE THING you can do today to begin living a life of significance?

A Heart of Courage

As usually happens, when God began to touch people's hearts, Satan came rushing in. As Paul and Silas went away from the crowds to pray, a demon-possessed slave girl started to follow them. When Paul healed the girl of that evil spirit, her masters were furious. Without her fortune-telling abilities, the men made no money. So they started a public campaign against the preachers. Paul and Silas were beaten and thrown in prison.

Can you imagine how Lydia felt when she heard the news of Paul and Silas? It all started so peacefully and grew with such joy, and then *bam!* The prison doors slammed shut on those who'd just led her to Christ and this new wonderful life. Lydia didn't know about the miracles that would soon take place, but she stayed faithful.

In prison, when Paul and Silas began to sing hymns of praise, God sent an earthquake that shook open the prison doors. The jailor heard the praise and now felt the quake. He asked, "What must I do to be saved?" Paul and Silas led the man to Christ.

Acts 16:40 tells us that the first place Paul went when he left the prison was to Lydia's house. She had gathered other believers there, and she was ready and waiting to minister to Paul and Silas. This lady was no fair-weather Christian. She didn't run scared. Instead, she prepared to help in the cause.

When Lydia opened her home, she showed that she cared about others finding eternal life as she did. She cultivated a place and opportunities for lost people to hear the gospel and to find Christ. What are you doing to make this happen?

GROUP DISCUSSION

What can you do to make your youth group such a place of hospitality?

A Heart That Influences

The church at Philippi was the first church in Europe. About ten years after he led Lydia to Christ, Paul wrote to the church that had started in her home: "I thank my God upon every remembrance of you, always in every prayer of mine making request for you all with joy, for your fellowship in the gospel from the first day until now, being confident of this very thing, that He who has begun a good work in you will complete it until the day of Jesus Christ" (Philippians 1:3–6).

What began with one woman's tender, open heart for God had now become a thriving Christian passionate community. Paul wrote to them with fond memories and with gratitude, for this once-small band of believers had ministered to him with financial gifts and encouragement over the years.

The influence didn't stop with Paul or with the city of Philippi, because their "good work" continues until the day Christ returns through the writings of the book of Philippians. Originally written to that church, Paul's letter to the Philippians was given also for us that we might be strengthened, encouraged, and motivated to live joyfully and skillfully in this present age.

FUSE BOX

A tender heart and tough resolve builds a reputation, builds a church, and brings people to Christ.

NOTES

PRIVATE WORLD DEVOTIONS

MONDAY: See it. Read the surrounding passages or chapter for the Key Scripture so that you can get an understanding of the background and context. This helps you to really *see* the verse.

TUESDAY: Hear it. Read the daily Key Scripture and/or surrounding passage out loud, putting your name in, if applicable. For example, <u>John</u> *can do all things through Christ. Thieves have come to destroy* <u>John</u>, *but Jesus has come that* <u>John</u> *might have eternal life.*

WEDNESDAY: Write it. Write the verse and then what it says about:

+ *Others:* Respond, serve, and love as Jesus would.

+ *Me:* Specific attitudes, choices, or habits.

+ *God:* His love, mercy, holiness, peace, joy, etc.

PRIVATE WORLD JOURNAL

*I am grateful for—I praise you for—I am
feeling—I am thinking—I need help with*

PRIVATE WORLD DEVOTIONS *(Continued)*

THURSDAY: Memorize it. Take the verse with you—write it on a card or put it in your phone, iPod, or PDA. Go over it throughout the day so that it begins to *live* in your heart and mind.

FRIDAY: Pray it. Personalize the verse as you pray for yourself or for others or in praise to God. To pray is literally "to think about." Try thinking out loud or writing in your **PRIVATE WORLD JOURNAL.**

SATURDAY: Share it. Ask the Lord to bring someone to mind or in your path today who needs good news. Don't be shy—just let it out! Whether you IM, write, text, tell, or send it, the joy of God's Word will flow from your heart into theirs.

PRAYER REQUESTS

Date	Name	Need	Answer

PRIVATE WORLD JOURNAL

I am grateful for—I praise you for—I am feeling—I am thinking—I need help with

NOTES

CHAPTER 6

KEEP THE DREAM ALIVE
JOSEPH

KEY SCRIPTURE

But as for you, you meant evil against me; but God meant it for good, in order to bring it about as it is this day, to save many people alive.

—Genesis 50:20

COULD THIS BE YOU?

Liz's childhood was far from carefree as she watched her mother struggle with schizophrenia, lived with her parents' drug abuse, and was never sure if there would be food for her and her sister. Around the age of ten, Liz became the "parent" in her family, taking care of her mom and dad. Then her mother died of AIDS, her father left with her sister, and Liz was left to fend for herself. At the age of fifteen, Liz was homeless.

> A life of significance is one that keeps Christ as the center and at the top of all priorities.

Just surviving would have been a triumph, but Liz wanted more. "I always knew there was something inside me worth exploring," says Liz.[1] Chris, a young man who had left home as a teenager, became Liz's closest friend, and together they found food and sometimes found shelter. But Liz also looked for an opportunity to finish high school. Chris wasn't interested; so on her own, Liz enrolled in a program that would allow her to obtain a diploma.

After two years of living on the streets and studying on the subway, Liz received her high school diploma. Based on her grades, determination, and example of courage, the *New York Times* awarded her with a full scholarship to Harvard. Liz Murray is now a national speaker who shares her story of hope with others.

She remains friends with Chris and a few others she met while homeless, although their lives have taken opposite paths. Chris is "still living on friends' couches," Liz says. "It's sometimes hard sharing with my friends all the things I'm doing now. It's especially hard with Chris, since we had a parallel journey at one point in time." [2]

WHY KNOW IT?

✦ In a given year, the U.S. Patent and Trademark Office will grant over 170,000 patents and register or reissue 120,000 trademarks.[3] That means someone receives a patent grant every three minutes or registers a trademark every five minutes.[4]

✦ Close to 175,000 books are published each year.[5]

✦ Over 6,000 new music albums are released each year.[6]

transfuse (trans FYOOZ) *to cause to pass from one to another; transmit*

Pastor Clarence Edward Macartney says that the biblical story of Joseph is filled with "every human passion—love and hate, ambition and glory, jealousy and fury. Tears of joy and grief are shed, garments are torn in anguish, it is a gripping saga of treachery and deception, betrayal and forgiveness."[7] It would make an outstanding daytime soap opera!

God has given us these great insights, experiences, and divine truths in the Old Testament to encourage us, to instruct us, and to warn us about how we should live our daily lives. What does Joseph have to do with teenagers today? He has a lot to tell us about dreaming and staying on track. He was misunderstood, ridiculed, tested, wrongfully accused and punished, betrayed, and lied to. Can you relate?

Through it all, Joseph lived a life of integrity and forgiveness with a goal of glorifying God. "He lived high above the all too common reactions of rage, resentment, and revenge. He became one of 'God's greats.'"[8]

Now Joseph had a dream, and he told it to his brothers; and they hated him even more. So he said to them, "Please hear this dream which I have dreamed: There we were, binding sheaves in the field. Then behold, my sheaf arose and also stood upright; and indeed your sheaves stood all around and bowed down to my sheaf." And his brothers said to him, "Shall you indeed reign over us? Or shall you indeed have dominion over us?" So they hated him even more for his dreams and for his words. **—Genesis 37:5–8**

We meet Joseph as a young man, probably about seventeen years old. From the very beginning, he had a dream to be used of the Lord to do something great. We know that Joseph's brothers despised him because his father loved him more than all the other brothers.

So when Joseph bragged to them about his dream in which his brothers were bowing down to him, it was the last straw. Maybe he should have kept quiet; certainly he could have at least shared without boasting. His attitude was a bit off, but on the positive side, he had a dream at a young age, and he was enthusiastic about it.

infuse (in FYOOZ) : to cause to be permeated with something (as a principle or quality) that alters usually for the better

Have a Big Dream to Live For

In Joseph's dream, he would become a ruler over all the other brothers. Although this seems like an arrogant dream, we have to applaud Joseph for believing such a big dream. Someone else might have said, "That sounds too hard. There will be too much and too many against me." To do something great for God, you have to believe that God truly will use you in a way beyond all human possibility. This is not arrogance or boasting but a sure purpose in living and a priority in how you use your time.

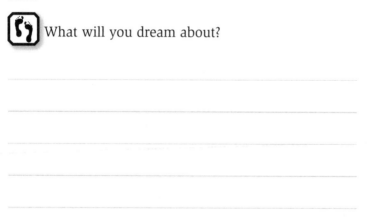 What will you dream about?

+ Dream big about how God wants to use you to change your school.

+ Dream about what you will do with your life, your career, and your calling.

+ Dream big enough to go on mission trips around the world, and don't let money, past, family history, or your hometown limit you from doing what God wants you to do.

Write one dream here:

_____

_____

_____

To see your dreams come true,

- ✦ feel more passion to pursue God's will than you do about anything else;

- ✦ make the dream more important than eating, breathing, or being with friends;

- ✦ stay motivated by the chance to influence and impact others;

- ✦ mentally and emotionally overrule the crowd culture or opinion.

Don't Let the Dream Die

So it came to pass, when Joseph had come to his brothers, that they stripped Joseph of his tunic, the tunic of many colors that was on him. Then they took him and cast him into a pit. And the pit was empty; there was no water in it. So Judah said to his brothers, "What profit is there if we kill our brother and conceal his blood? Come and let us sell him to the Ishmaelites, and let not our hand be upon him, for he is our brother and our flesh." And his brothers listened. **—Genesis 37:23–24, 26–27**

When God gives you a dream, it can only be unfulfilled if you allow it to be so. In Joseph's case, the obstacles were many. First, his brothers threw him in a ditch, then they changed their minds and sold him for twenty pieces of silver. That was a degrading stunt, but even more so when you realize that this was the price for a handicapped slave. They really didn't care how much they got; it was just about humiliating him.

 What obstacles do you face in obtaining your dream? (Circle all that apply, or fill in the blank)

✦ Lack of money, confidence, time

✦ What others say

✦ Spiritual fortitude

✦ Other:_____

What have your failures taught you? How have they made you a more capable leader?

_____

_____

_____

What ONE THING can you do to go around that obstacle?

_____

_____

_____

_____

Believe That Help Is on the Way

> *Then Midianite traders passed by; so the*
> *brothers pulled Joseph up and lifted him out*
> *of the pit, and sold him to the Ishmaelites*
> *for twenty shekels of silver. And they took*
> *Joseph to Egypt.* **—Genesis 37:28**

Joseph's dream had been thrown in the pit, but God sent a caravan to rescue it. He was taken to Egypt, where "the Lord made all he did to prosper" (Genesis 39:3). Perhaps Joseph thought that his dream was just about to come true now that he was finding success. It didn't all fit the original dream yet, but it gave him hope.

diffuse (di FYOOZ): to pour out and permit or cause to spread freely; to extend, scatter

Don't Live in the Moment

> *Now Joseph had been taken down to Egypt.*
> *And Potiphar, an officer of Pharaoh, captain*
> *of the guard, an Egyptian, bought him from*
> *the Ishmaelites who had taken him down*
> *there. The Lord was with Joseph, and he was*
> *a successful man; and he was in the house*
> *of his master the Egyptian. And his master*
> *saw that the Lord was with him and that the*
> *Lord made all he did to prosper in his hand.*
> *So Joseph found favor in his sight, and served*
> *him. Then he made him overseer of his house,*
> *and all that he had he put under his authority.*
> *And it came to pass after these things that his*
> *master's wife cast longing eyes on Joseph, and*
> *she said, "Lie with me."* **—Genesis 39:1–4, 7**

Joseph knew that the quickest way to lose focus on the dream was to allow himself to be drawn into immorality.

That's why when Potiphar's wife approached him, he was careful not to trample the dream.

Dreams deliver you from a life of insignificance, immorality, inconsistency, and injustices. Most people get disqualified because they allow the dream to die through giving in to sin or reacting to circumstances through anger or depression. So when Potiphar's wife tried to seduce him, Joseph responded, "Why would I give up my integrity and future for this one moment?"

That's the question each of us must ask in the moment of temptation. Is this one moment worth it? It never is.

Rarely do we plan to fail. Usually it happens "in the moment." Think about this week. Are there people, thoughts, or plans you need to deal with ahead of time so that you are not caught "in the moment"?

Live in the Future

Then Joseph's master took him and put him into the prison, a place where the king's prisoners were confined. And he was there in the prison. But the LORD was with Joseph and showed him mercy, and He gave him favor in the sight of the keeper of the prison. —**Genesis 39:20–21**

Because of the false accusation by Potiphar's wife, Joseph was banished to a dungeon. Once again, it looked like Joseph's dream was over, but it wasn't. It was just one more lesson for the journey.

What happens when you are in the dungeon? If you allow your dream to die, it becomes a place of dryness, doubt, depression, delay, and disqualifications.

Joseph learned not to dwell on the difficulty of the present, but to focus on the future. He knew by now that when one door closed, another would open if he was patient.

Joseph had to learn to serve before he could learn to lead. Every moment of life comes together to prepare you for the future.

You'll have to read the rest of the story to see how Joseph endured imprisonment, betrayal by friends, and long periods of waiting. But his dream did come true. In Genesis 41:39–40, Pharaoh praises Joseph, whom he promotes to the second-highest-ranking ruler in Egypt: "Inasmuch as God has shown you all this, there is no one as discerning and wise as you. You shall be over my house, and all my people shall be ruled according to your word; only in regard to the throne will I be greater than you."

> Success is the ability to go from one failure to another with no loss of enthusiasm.
> —Winston Churchill

And there it is, the fulfillment of the dream that God gave him so long ago as a teenager. Joseph was indeed ruler over a great many people, and his brothers did bow to him when they came to Egypt, asking for food.

Now that Joseph had power and the dream was fulfilled, how did it change him?

Pray for 50/20 Vision

> [Joseph said,] But as for you, you meant evil against me; but God meant it for good, in order to bring it about as it is this day, to save many people alive. —**Genesis 50:20**

As his brothers made their way to Joseph, the tables were turned. They were now at his mercy, and he held all power to destroy and humiliate them in any way he chose. But he did not; he could not. Joseph's dream gave him "50/20 vision" (based on Genesis 50:20) to see how all the experiences of his life had come together at this moment to fulfill the dream given by God.

"50/20 vision" causes you to:

✦ Praise God and speak of His goodness, even at the moment of possible revenge.

✦ Influence and bless your enemies as you demonstrate the love of Christ.

✦ Believe God will use for good whatever others mean to use against you.

WHAT MAKES A DREAMER?

 If you are captivated by the dream and controlled by the Dream Giver, it will be said of you, "Here comes the dreamer" and, "The Lord is with him."

A Dreamer Has a Sincere Private World

✦ Each time God revealed something to Joseph through a dream, He did so privately. It was up to Joseph to act on what God had shown him, because no one would know to ask him.

 Those who have a deep walk with God are known as "people of vision".

✦ Joseph was gifted, greatly blessed, and had a great relationship with God; however, he was still immature when he received his first dream. His commitment to the Lord was more important than his age.

If people around you say, "You're too young," focus on establishing habits in your private world—your inner life. You won't have to defend your public world because your godly habits will speak for themselves. By the way, how is your private world coming along?

A Dreamer Prepares for Obstacles

Joseph often found himself living with those who did not believe in his God. He was in Egypt, known for all its temptations and idols, but *he never allowed Egypt inside him*. He modeled that ordinary people can go through life without changing their moral values regardless of those around them.

✦ Don't give up on a dream even when obstacles come or circumstances change.

✦ Realize that today's actions impact tomorrow's goals.

Oftentimes, God gives us the dream or the vision to enable us to rise above the dungeon experiences of life. God gives us the vision before the difficulty so that when we need inspiration, it is already there.

✦ There will always be those who are jealous and treat you badly, those who laugh and don't support you, and those who don't understand you.

> For every pit Satan has, God has a caravan already on the way!

✦ Do you sometimes feel that you are in the minority at school or even at church? The journey of the dreamer is sometimes a lonely one.

A big dream gives you the 50/20 vision of other people—that God is the engineer of our circumstances, and we cannot retaliate or blame others for what He has allowed in our lives.

A Dreamer Is Changed by the Journey

When you have a dream worth living for, you are more than willing to keep going regardless. Through all his challenges and circumstances, Joseph journeyed from an arrogant youth to a compassionate adult.

The life of significance does not focus on the temporary, but thinks about the big picture. Have you ever stopped to look at a timeline of your life? Your teen years last about seven years, which is less than one tenth of your whole life span. Yet the choices you make in those seven years and the consequences that follow will be with you for a lifetime.

Birth Date   **Today**   **Day You Die**

History   Opportunity

FUSE BOX

Just imagine . . . if you could do anything, go anywhere, what would you do? If time were no limitation, if money were no object, if you could do anything, what would it be? Begin to pray, "Lord, I have no limitations other than Your will. Call me to Yourself and to the dream You have for me."

NOTES

To rule others, you
have to learn to first
rule yourself.

PRIVATE WORLD DEVOTIONS

MONDAY: See it. Read the surrounding passages or chapter for the Key Scripture so that you can get an understanding of the background and context. This helps you to really *see* the verse.

TUESDAY: Hear it. Read the daily Key Scripture and/or surrounding passage out loud, putting your name in, if applicable. For example, <u>John</u> *can do all things through Christ. Thieves have come to destroy* <u>John</u>, *but Jesus has come that* <u>John</u> *might have eternal life.*

WEDNESDAY: Write it. Write the verse and then what it says about:

✦ *Others:* Respond, serve, and love as Jesus would.

✦ *Me:* Specific attitudes, choices, or habits.

✦ *God:* His love, mercy, holiness, peace, joy, etc.

PRIVATE WORLD JOURNAL

I am grateful for—I praise you for—I am feeling—I am thinking—I need help with

PRIVATE WORLD DEVOTIONS *(Continued)*

THURSDAY: Memorize it. Take the verse with you—write it on a card or put it in your phone, iPod, or PDA. Go over it throughout the day so that it begins to *live* in your heart and mind.

FRIDAY: Pray it. Personalize the verse as you pray for yourself or for others or in praise to God. To pray is literally "to think about." Try thinking out loud or writing in your **PRIVATE WORLD JOURNAL.**

SATURDAY: Share it. Ask the Lord to bring someone to mind or in your path today who needs good news. Don't be shy—just let it out! Whether you IM, write, text, tell, or send it, the joy of God's Word will flow from your heart into theirs.

PRAYER REQUESTS

Date	Name	Need	Answer

PRIVATE WORLD JOURNAL

I am grateful for—I praise you for—I am feeling—I am thinking—I need help with

NOTES

CHAPTER 7

TURN PAIN INTO COMPASSION

ESTHER

KEY SCRIPTURE

And we know that all things work together for good to those who love God, to those who are the called according to His purpose.

—Romans 8:28

COULD THIS BE YOU?

In the picturesque tidewater basin of the Virginia coast, three young boys were born in stair-step fashion. Soon after the third son was born, the mother was stricken with cancer. Striving to take care of three children age three and below, fighting the onset of cancer, and trying to cope with an alcoholic husband was more than she could handle. When her youngest son was eleven months of age, she could take it no longer and died.

> A man is a hero, not because he is braver than anyone else, but because he is brave for ten minutes longer.
>
> —Ralph Waldo Emerson

The father now found himself responsible not only for a military career, but for raising three small children. There were short periods where the boys seemed fine, but many times the father saw them as a nuisance. The responsibility and demands were more than he wanted to face. Compared to raising three preschoolers, the military was a breeze, and the boys got in the way of his drinking.

Growing tired of the boys, the father left them in various homes so he could have a break for a while. When he needed to feel good about himself or to ensure that he received financial aid for his dependent children, he would grab them back. Thus the cycle began: hand off the kids and get some breathing room, drag the kids back when you need them, and find yourself forced to fit into a parent's role.

The seemingly endless cycle occurred repeatedly—until finally the father gave up the boys for good. They were passed from hand to hand and house to house, all the way from Virginia to southern Illinois, where they found themselves deposited temporarily with another family who was willing to take them in—at least for a short while.

A young couple in southern Illinois, who longed for children of their own but were unable to conceive, heard about the three "unwanted" boys. They approached the home where the boys were being kept and offered to help. The woman told them that the older two boys had already been taken by another couple, but if they wanted the youngest, they could have him. The young couple found the little boy playing in a back bedroom. It was obvious he had not been washed for days and had been sitting in diapers that had long since needed changing . . . despite the fact that he was well past the time when a child could be out of diapers. What was worse, the little guy was covered with sores.

> And we know that all things work together for good to those who love God, to those who are the called according to His purpose.
> —Romans 8:28

The young wife grabbed the small child up in her arms—his sores staining her new dress—and with her husband, they left the house with their new son. The young couple, neither of whom finished high school, would go on to care for and raise the little boy. By their example, the boy learned about Jesus and became a very strong Christian.

The boy, Bob Reccord, would grow up to become the president of the North American Mission Board for the Southern Baptist Convention. Today, he leads an organization that focuses on providing resources to families in need and sharing the love of Christ.

WHY KNOW IT?

✦ "Not succeeding in life or being a failure" ranks as one of teenagers' top five fears.[1]

✦ Common responses from teens who were asked what they were most afraid of include: "Making mistakes that will mess up my life"; "Not being successful"; "Not measuring up"; "Not getting into a good college"; "I'll close doors on myself and find myself in a position where I can't succeed because of something I'm doing right now"; "Not leaving a mark."[2]

✦ 87 percent of teens believe there is an overall purpose for their life.[3]

transfuse (trans FYOOZ) : to cause to pass from one to another; transmit

We never know what lessons our daily lives will teach us, but we can be sure that God does not waste a moment. Just as He used the pain Christ endured on the Cross to give us eternal life, He uses the pain and disappointment of our lives to shape us into compassionate, caring people.

If you are going through a difficult or painful circumstance, be encouraged by James 1:2–4, which says, "Count it all joy when you fall into various trials, knowing that the testing of your faith produces patience. But let patience have its perfect work, that you may be perfect and complete, lacking nothing."

The good news is that God loves you so much that nothing you endure or go through is wasted. He makes all of it into a complete work.

*When the heart of the king was merry with
wine, he commanded . . . seven eunuchs who
served in the presence of King Ahasuerus, to
bring Queen Vashti before the king, wearing
her royal crown, in order to show her beauty
to the people and the officials, for she was
beautiful to behold. But Queen Vashti refused
to come at the king's command brought by his
eunuchs; therefore the king was furious, and his
anger burned within him. —Esther 1:10–12*

After a six-month party of drunkenness, Xerxes decided
to display his beautiful wife, Vashti, for all the nations
to view. She refused, and Xerxes immediately banished
her. To save face for his ridiculous mistake, he sent out
to find a new wife by collecting all the attractive virgin
women from around the land. Thus, Esther, a woman of
great beauty, was found and brought to be in the running
for the role of the new queen.

infuse (in FYOOZ) : to cause to be permeated with something
(as a principle or quality) that alters usually for the better

*In Shushan the citadel there was a certain Jew
whose name was Mordecai the son of Jair, the
son of Shimei, the son of Kish, a Benjamite.
Kish had been carried away from Jerusalem
with the captives who had been captured with
Jeconiah king of Judah, whom Nebuchadnezzar
the king of Babylon had carried away. And
Mordecai had brought up Hadassah, that
is, Esther, his uncle's daughter, for she had
neither father nor mother. —Esther 2:5–7*

God Uses Our Pain to Make Us Compassionate Toward Others

Things didn't start well for Esther. Her parents died when she was a young girl, and she went to live with her cousin, Mordecai. This deep sadness within her was the beginning of a compassionate spirit for the pain and needs of others. Mordecai raised Esther, and he loved her as his own daughter. Mordecai knew firsthand the loneliness she felt, since his great-grandfather was carried into exile from Jerusalem by Nebuchadnezzar, king of Babylon.

> Bitterness imprisons life; love releases it.
> —Harry Emerson Fosdick

Together, this new little family lived under the reign of King Xerxes. We can be sure that Mordecai taught Esther love and compassion from the lessons of his own life.

Esther appears in the Bible as a woman of deep faith, courage, patriotism, and caution. She was a daughter who respected her adopted father and did not allow the pain of her childhood to cause bitterness. Instead, she was tenderhearted and caring.

God Uses Our Pain to Mold Our Inner Spirit

> *Now the young woman pleased him, and she obtained his favor; so he readily gave beauty preparations to her, besides her allowance. Then seven choice maidservants were provided for her from the king's palace, and he moved her and her maidservants to the best place in the house of the women. The king loved Esther more than all the other women, and she obtained grace and favor in his sight more than all the virgins; so he set the royal crown upon her head and made her queen instead of Vashti.* —**Esther 2:17**

Instead of complaining about a difficult situation, write thoughts of gratitude to the Lord in your journal. Focus on His promise that He is working all things together for good. (See Romans 8:28.)

Scripture tells us that Esther was beautiful outwardly, but the spirit that she exhibited to others must have been so lovely that it set her apart. We are told that "many young women" were brought to the king; but of all the women there, only Esther "obtained grace and favor in his sight" (2:8, 17). The Hebrew word translated "favor" in this verse is *chen*, meaning "pleasant" and "precious."

Esther's combined inner and outer beauty was so outstanding that, out of all the virgins brought throughout the land, the king chose her to be his queen.

GROUP DISCUSSION

Which is more important: how people view your body, clothes, hair, and appearance, or your inner spirit?

Which do you spend more time on?

What do you focus on when you look at others? Is it the same as above?

_____

_____

_____

Now think about this. Here is a king of great power. He has had one queen so beautiful that her name, *Vashti*, literally meant "beauty." He banished his previous wife because of a decision he made in a drunken state. Now he is looking for a new wife. What kind of woman do you suppose he would choose?

Common sense would say he was looking for someone who would not mind the drunken choices, who would not mind being treated like a possession, and would not demand respect. Because of his previous decision with Vashti, the women may have talked among themselves about ways to be chosen. They probably discussed body image, facial gestures, and how to get the king to notice them. This was huge! Being chosen as queen meant power, wealth, servants, luxury, and status. What woman wouldn't want to be queen?

Have you ever been tempted to change yourself—your dress, actions, morals—in order to be "chosen" by the popular crowd?

God Uses Pain to Build Resolve and Clarify Our Values

You would think that an orphan, raised in a poor home, would do anything to attain a royal position. But not Esther. Having few material possessions to hold on to, Esther learned to value courage, resolve, and kindness instead. She built her life around these qualities, and when the time came for proving who you were, she showed a display like none of the other women. This pompous and powerful king chose Esther because she found "grace and favor in his sight."

He didn't say she invoked lust, was gorgeous, or flattered him with words. Scripture tells us that he "loved" what he saw within her, and that was "grace and favor" (Esther 2:17). Two Hebrew words for "favor" are used by the king. The first is the same "favor" that the custodian of the woman used. But then he adds a second word, the Hebrew *checed*, implying a piety—that is, a modest goodness.

So different was this modest spirit of kindness and goodness in Esther that it caused her to stand out above all other women, and it invoked a love for her spirit in this otherwise very selfish king. There is the true power of a person, their inner testimony. Modest is hottest!

Don't be fooled by believing you can fool people with actions, words, and behavior. Either what you have in Christ is so real, so amazing, so pure, and so different from every one else that you stand out and draw others to you, or you are just another guy, just another girl.

diffuse (di FYOOZ)**:** to pour out and permit or cause to spread freely; to extend, scatter

For Such a Time As This

All of the moments of Esther's life worked together to make her who she was and to bring her into this position of prestige. She went from being the adopted daughter of one of the king's servants to the elevated, chosen queen.

GROUP DISCUSSION

Discuss Dr. Reccord's story at the beginning of this chapter. What do you think God might be preparing you to do?

Write two possibilities:

1.

2.

> *Then Haman said to King Ahasuerus, "There is a certain people scattered and dispersed among the people in all the provinces of your kingdom; their laws are different from all other people's, and they do not keep the king's laws. Therefore it is not fitting for the king to let them remain.* —**Esther 3:8**

The "certain people" Haman referred to were the Jews. Haman wanted them destroyed because Jews would not bow down to him. The Jews were about to be annihilated—unless a heroine could be found to save them.

The courage Esther developed as a child was about to be multiplied. Out of anger, the wicked Haman deceived Xerxes into writing a decree that all Jews should be killed. Once it was decreed and the king gave his signet ring as an oath, nothing could undo the deed. The Jews were to face certain death. But, enter Esther, the beautiful, poised, compassionate queen, who just happened to be a Jew.

There was one small problem. Esther could not approach the king without being asked, and to enter without his permission could bring about death for her.

Her cousin Mordecai took her aside and explained that she must do the thing she did not want to do. He let her know that if she didn't stand up for the Jewish people that God could use someone else. Then he challenged her: "Yet who knows whether you have come to the kingdom for such a time as this?" (Esther 4:14).

When I honestly care about others, I don't give consideration to the sacrifice I might be asked to make.

Think about your campus, church group, and community. Have you ever wondered why you are in that particular place? You are there because God placed you there. As mediocrity and evil abound, ask yourself, "Have I been placed here for such a time as this?"

It's time for you to step up!

What ONE THING can you do to begin to make a difference in your circle of influence?

When can you start?

How will you do it?

> The significant life begins with a transformed mind. Think about how to continuously express the mind of Christ to other people. It's not just talk; it's a lifestyle.

Who can help you?

We know that, out of great compassion for her people, Esther did approach the king and risked his anger. And remember, so far, his track record was anything but love and patience! Now this is an amazing story and one you must completely read during your quiet time this week.

✦ God blessed the faith of Esther and *favored* her.

✦ God softened Xerxes' heart so that he listened to her request and worked to bring about peace.

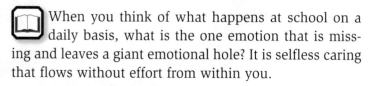 When you think of what happens at school on a daily basis, what is the one emotion that is missing and leaves a giant emotional hole? It is selfless caring that flows without effort from within you.

✦ When you exhibit this kind of heart, people will come to you regardless of how you look on the outside.

✦ When you live this kind of love, you are willing to risk reputation and give of yourself in an effort to rescue others.

✦ When you understand that God has called you to a unique purpose, you can look at the world and say, "What can I do to make a difference?"

FUSE BOX

A life of significance is centered on a unique purpose planned by God *for such a time as this* and understands that every event in life works toward this purpose.

NOTES

PRIVATE WORLD DEVOTIONS

MONDAY: See it. Read the surrounding passages or chapter for the Key Scripture so that you can get an understanding of the background and context. This helps you to really *see* the verse.

TUESDAY: Hear it. Read the daily Key Scripture and/or surrounding passage out loud, putting your name in, if applicable. For example, <u>John</u> *can do all things through Christ. Thieves have come to destroy* <u>John</u>, *but Jesus has come that* <u>John</u> *might have eternal life.*

WEDNESDAY: Write it. Write the verse and then what it says about:

- ✦ *Others:* Respond, serve, and love as Jesus would.
- ✦ *Me:* Specific attitudes, choices, or habits.
- ✦ *God:* His love, mercy, holiness, peace, joy, etc.

PRIVATE WORLD JOURNAL

I am grateful for—I praise you for—I am feeling—I am thinking—I need help with

PRIVATE WORLD DEVOTIONS *(Continued)*

THURSDAY: Memorize it. Take the verse with you—write it on a card or put it in your phone, iPod, or PDA. Go over it throughout the day so that it begins to *live* in your heart and mind.

FRIDAY: Pray it. Personalize the verse as you pray for yourself or for others or in praise to God. To pray is literally "to think about." Try thinking out loud or writing in your **PRIVATE WORLD JOURNAL.**

SATURDAY: Share it. Ask the Lord to bring someone to mind or in your path today who needs good news. Don't be shy—just let it out! Whether you IM, write, text, tell, or send it, the joy of God's Word will flow from your heart into theirs.

PRAYER REQUESTS

Date	Name	Need	Answer

PRIVATE WORLD JOURNAL

I am grateful for—I praise you for—I am feeling—I am thinking—I need help with

NOTES

CHAPTER 8

START A REVOLUTION
JOHN THE BAPTIST

KEY SCRIPTURE

There was a man sent from God, whose name was John. This man came for a witness, to bear witness of the Light, that all through him might believe.
—**John 1:6–7**

COULD THIS BE YOU?

Telemachus, being a monk, spent most of his life secluded away from the crowd, usually immersed with the disciplines of studying and praying. In fact, he probably knew very little about the world outside of his own. There came a day when he felt called to travel to Rome and minister to the people there. It was during the days of the Roman Empire, and it would be quite a change of pace from what he had been accustomed to, but young Telemachus obeyed by gathering all of his belongings and beginning the trek to Rome.

He arrived in Rome during the middle of a holiday festival. People were everywhere, vendors on every corner, and swarms of people in the streets. Deciding to follow the crowd and observe the festivities, Telemachus ended up in the Coliseum, which scholars say would most likely have been filled during the holiday season for the popular chariot races and Coliseum games. Telemachus watched as the gladiators battled to gruesome death after death in front of an audience of up to eighty thousand people.

Finally, he had seen enough, and he climbed down to the Coliseum's amphitheater, where the gladiators battled. Moved to anger and then action, the pious monk entered the arena alone, pushing aside the fighting gladiators and shouting, "In the name of Christ, forbear!" The crowds, disappointed in the disturbance of their entertainment, yelled for the games and the fighting to continue. The gladiators battled Telemachus out of the way, but he would not give up. He again tried to stop the gladiators from battling, urging the gladiators to stop. The crowd became furious and began demanding that Telemachus be killed as well.

The commander of the games, overseeing the series of events that had unfolded before him, heard the plea of the crowd and gave the thumbs-down, signaling the execution order for the monk. With his last breath, Telemachus proclaimed in his loudest voice, "In the name of Christ, forbear!" His lifeless body fell to the ground as the gladiator struck the deadly blow. It was 80,000 to 1.

Then, a strange thing happened. An odd silence fell across the Coliseum, and the crowd became still. One by one, the eyes of the crowd began to be opened as they finally realized what had happened. Grasping the horror of the sport they had once celebrated, one at a time, people began to leave the arena until the entire Coliseum was deserted. It would be the last gladiatorial battle fought in the Roman Coliseum.

> It's more than revolutions that clear the road to new and better days. It is someone's soul inspired and ablaze.
> —Boris Pasternak

Telemachus, the isolated monk, didn't have any political standing, great fame, or wealth.

He was a man who held strongly to his convictions, was available to be used by God, and impacted Roman society forever by simply starting a revolution with the power of one.

WHY KNOW IT?

✦ Only 4 in 10 teenagers are excited about being active in church.[1]

✦ 24 percent of people age 16 to 24 volunteer their time.[2]

✦ Making a difference in people's lives ranks in the top ten goals teenagers have for their lives.[3]

✦ Teens who are at the top of their class are twice as likely to volunteer their time for charity or social service activities.[4]

transfuse (trans FYOOZ); to cause to pass from one to another; transmit

God has made each of us with a unique purpose, and that is why we long to find a cause to live for, to pour ourselves into, and to provide a sense of accomplishment. Discovering our life purpose starts at home and extends to the church.

✦ A revolutionary works to make his or her family a success.

✦ A revolutionary will choose as a priority of life to become involved with the vision the youth pastor and pastor have for the church and youth ministry and wholeheartedly commit to serving.

Ask your youth leader for ONE THING you can do to support him or her this week.

Write it here:

_____

_____

_____

The synergy of working together becomes fuel to accomplish great things for God. Hebrews 10:24 encourages us: "Let us consider one another in order to stir up love and good works."

Again, the next day, John stood with two of his disciples. And looking at Jesus as He walked, he said, "Behold the Lamb of God!" The two disciples heard him speak, and they followed Jesus. Then Jesus turned, and seeing them following, said to them, "What do you seek?" They said to Him, "Rabbi" (which is to say, when translated, Teacher), "where are You staying?" He said to them, "Come and see." They came and saw where He was staying, and remained with Him that day (now it was about the tenth hour). One of the two who heard John speak, and followed Him, was Andrew, Simon Peter's brother. He first found his own brother Simon, and said to him, "We have found the Messiah" (which is translated, the Christ). And he brought him to Jesus. Now when Jesus looked at him, He said, "You are Simon the son of Jonah. You shall be called Cephas" (which is translated, A Stone). The following day Jesus wanted to go to Galilee, and He found Philip and said to him, "Follow Me." Now Philip

> *was from Bethsaida, the city of Andrew and
> Peter. Philip found Nathaniel and said to him,
> "We have found Him of whom Moses in the
> law, and also the prophets, wrote—Jesus of
> Nazareth, the son of Joseph."* —**John 1:35–45**

The John mentioned in this passage was John the Baptist. He was "a man sent from God" (John 1:6). He had disciples, and when he came into the room there was a buzz. Even though he preached and baptized way out in the desert far from the city of Jerusalem, John the Baptist attracted great crowds of all types—soldiers, common people, business leaders. He was a revolutionary who gave his life in order to prepare the way for the people to meet the Messiah. What an honor that must have been!

infuse (in FYOOZ)¸ to cause to be permeated with something (as a principle or quality) that alters usually for the better

Understand Your Call

> *There was a man sent from God, whose name
> was John. This man came for a witness, to
> bear witness of the Light, that all through him
> might believe. He was not that Light, but was
> sent to bear witness of that Light. That was the
> true Light which give light to every man coming
> into the world. John bore witness of Him and
> cried out, saying, "This was He of whom I said,
> 'He who comes after me is preferred before me,
> for He was before me.'"* —**John 1:6–9, 15**

Although John the Baptist's message drew a crowd and many people followed him, he was never so arrogant to think that he was the reason for all the excitement. He understood that his ministry was to prepare the way for Jesus, who was much greater than he, and to share Christ's message.

✦ A revolutionary prepares the way for others to see God's work; he or she doesn't draw attention to self. As John the Baptist said of Jesus, "He must increase, but I must decrease" (John 3:30).

✦ You can't lead others if you don't know where you are going. Work on having a clear personal mission first.

Before you continue on your life journey, take a moment to smooth the road. Is there anything in your life that would be a pothole, detour, or boulder to reaching others for Christ?

Gain a Reputation

> Now this is the testimony of John, when the Jews sent priests and Levites from Jerusalem to ask him, "Who are you?" He confessed, and did not deny, but confessed, "I am not the Christ." And they asked him, "What then? Are you Elijah?" He said, "I am not." "Are you the Prophet?" And he answered, "No." Then they said to him, "Who are you, that we may give an answer to those who sent us? What do you say about yourself?" He said: "I am 'The voice of one crying in the wilderness: "Make straight the way of the Lord," ' as the prophet Isaiah said." —**John 1:19–23**

John the Baptist gained a reputation for stirring things up. He did not care what others might say or how he looked or whether he would be popular. He was born with a purpose, and he intended to fulfill it.

The Christian who believes that he or she has been born to a purpose looks at the state of the world and says, "This ought not to be, and I have to do something about it. I can make a difference."

GROUP DISCUSSION

Is there anything you have seen at your school or youth group that "ought not to be"?

+ What can you do?

_____

_____

_____

_____

Esther's beauty brought her to the citadel, but her kind and caring personality got her into the finals.

+ When will you do it?

_____

_____

_____

+ Who will help you?

_____

_____

_____

✦ How will you do it?

_____

_____

_____

_____

_____

Start a Chain Reaction

John's bold testimony to Jesus as the Messiah in John 1:35–37 resulted in Andrew's conversion. Andrew's testimony in turn led his brother Cephas, or Simon, to Christ. Simon's name was later changed to Peter, and you know the rest of that story. In verse 42, Jesus called Phillip on the Sea of Galilee, and he also testified of the Messiah.

Could a chain reaction start on your campus as you *prepare the way*? Begin this week to pray for that one person you can win to Christ who might begin the reaction.

Who is it?

_____

_____

_____

When will you pray specifically?

_____

_____

_____

diffuse (di FYOOZ) : to pour out and permit or cause to spread freely; to extend, scatter

Be Confident in Your Mission

When you know what your mission is—Christ—then you don't have to pretend to be who you are not. Are you Messiah? Are you Elijah? A prophet? No! People might try to categorize you into a defined box, but don't let them. You don't have to play every game that comes along, every fad, or trend.

When you swim at the beach, you know that the greatest danger is getting accidentally caught in a current. Without anything to hold on to or an anchor to keep you where you started, you can easily be swept way out to sea.

 A definite mission provides internal anchors that keep you from drifting.

> *For this is he who was spoken of by the prophet Isaiah, saying: "The voice of one crying in the wilderness: "Prepare the way of the LORD; make His paths straight." —***Matthew 3:3**

Be a Voice and Not an Echo

John was not like anyone in the crowd. He lived differently, dressed differently, spoke differently, and gave not one thought to doing otherwise.

The crowd is the preferred place of most students. They follow whatever the crowd does—repeating lyrics from a song, dressing like celebrities, living by movie lines, or buying whatever is popular at the moment.

Who do you want people to see when they look at you? Do you want to remind them of someone else, or do you want to remind them of Christ?

✦ John stayed true to the mission, and the crowd came to him.

Think about your three best friends: Would you characterize each as a voice or an echo?

1. _____

2. _____

3. _____

What about yourself?

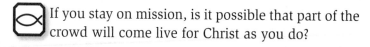

If you stay on mission, is it possible that part of the crowd will come live for Christ as you do?

Live for Something Worth Dying For

And when John had heard in prison about the works of Christ, he sent two of his disciples and said to Him, "Are You the Coming One, or do we look for another?" Jesus answered and said to them, "Go and tell John the things which you hear and see: The blind see and the lame walk; the lepers are cleansed and the deaf hear; the dead are raised up and the poor have the gospel preached to them. And blessed is he who is not offended because of Me." —Matthew 11:2–6

Even when he was in prison, John was still focused. He had given his time, energy, and reputation to prepare the way for Jesus. Now he was thrown into prison for doing so, and he wanted some assurances. He sent word to Jesus: "Are You the Coming One?" (v. 3). Jesus, in His infinite patience, answered, "Go and tell John what you see . . ." (v. 4).

Once John knew that the cause was sure, he was ready to die for it. John the Baptist was eventually beheaded at the request of one of Herod's daughters because John had objected to their sin. Until the very end of his life, John stayed committed—no matter the cost— to becoming more like Christ.

Likewise, on an ordinary spring day, seventeen-year-old Cassie Bernall faced a classmate who pointed a gun to her head. He asked, "Do you believe in God?" Cassie answered without hesitation, "Yes." Then she was shot dead.

The story of Cassie's death is told on numerous Web pages, but just as powerful is the story of her life. Cassie lived what she believed, and her one-word answer has given courage to thousands of students.

[FUSE BOX]

When you know who you are in Christ and what your sure call is, you can prepare the way for others to see the Savior.

PRIVATE WORLD DEVOTIONS

MONDAY: See it. Read the surrounding passages or chapter for the Key Scripture so that you can get an understanding of the background and context. This helps you to really *see* the verse.

TUESDAY: Hear it. Read the daily Key Scripture and/or surrounding passage out loud, putting your name in, if applicable. For example, <u>John</u> *can do all things through Christ. Thieves have come to destroy* <u>John</u>*, but Jesus has come that* <u>John</u> *might have eternal life.*

WEDNESDAY: Write it. Write the verse and then what it says about:

- ✦ *Others:* Respond, serve, and love as Jesus would.
- ✦ *Me:* Specific attitudes, choices, or habits.
- ✦ *God:* His love, mercy, holiness, peace, joy, etc.

PRIVATE WORLD JOURNAL

*I am grateful for—I praise you for—I am
feeling—I am thinking—I need help with*

PRIVATE WORLD DEVOTIONS *(Continued)*

THURSDAY: Memorize it. Take the verse with you—write it on a card or put it in your phone, iPod, or PDA. Go over it throughout the day so that it begins to *live* in your heart and mind.

FRIDAY: Pray it. Personalize the verse as you pray for yourself or for others or in praise to God. To pray is literally "to think about." Try thinking out loud or writing in your **PRIVATE WORLD JOURNAL.**

SATURDAY: Share it. Ask the Lord to bring someone to mind or in your path today who needs good news. Don't be shy—just let it out! Whether you IM, write, text, tell, or send it, the joy of God's Word will flow from your heart into theirs.

PRAYER REQUESTS

Date	Name	Need	Answer

PRIVATE WORLD JOURNAL

I am grateful for—I praise you for—I am feeling—I am thinking—I need help with

Notes

CHAPTER 1—KEEP A QUIET TIME: DANIEL

1. A. C. Green, "Faithful On and Off the Court," *Vital Signs Ministries* (March 1994). http://www.vitalsignsministries.org/vsma.html (accessed 6 July 2005).

2. Ibid.

3. "Frequently Asked Questions: A. C. Green," ClubAC. http://www.clubac.com/ask/default.asp?DocumentID = 390 (accessed 6 July 2005).

4. "Speak Out," ClubAC. http://www.clubac.com/abstinence/default.asp?TopicID = 4 (accessed 19 July 2005).

5. "Frequently Asked Questions: A.C. Green," ClubAC.

6. "Few U.S. Protestant Teens Regularly Read the Bible," National Study of Youth and Religion (23 June 2004). http://www.youthandreligion.org/news/2004-0623.html (accessed 6 July 2005).

7. "Annual Study Reveals America is Spiritually Stagnant," The Barna Group (5 March 2001). http://www.barna.org/FlexPage.aspx?Page = BarnaUpdate&BarnaUpdateID = 84 (accessed 6 July 2005).

8. "My Journey Home," PBS (7April 2004). http://www.pbs.org/weta/myjourneyhome/teachers/literacy.html (accessed 18 July 2005).

9. Ann Landers, "Where Our Time Goes During Our Working Careers," *Houston Chronicle* (30 August 1996). http://www.chron.com/content/chronicle/features/96/09/02/annlanders.html (accessed 18 July 2005).

10. www.bible-history.com

CHAPTER 2—LIVE A LIFE OF WORSHIP: DAVID

1. "Band Member Bios: Mac Powell," Third Day. http://www.thirdday.com/wmac.html (accessed 20 July 2005).

2. Todd Hertz, "No Longer Just a Rock Band," *Christianity Today* (4 February 2002). http://www.christianitytoday.com/ct/2002/002/34.88.html (accessed 20 July 2005).

3. "Third Day," Christianity Today. http://www.christianitytoday.com/music/artists/thirdday.html (accessed 20 July 2005).

4. Todd Hertz, "No Longer Just a Rock Band."

5. Martin Cockroft, "The Heart of Worship," *Campus Life* (May/June 1999). http://www.christianitytoday.com/cl/9c6/9c6022.html (accessed 20 July 2005).

6. Ibid.

7. Steve Hanway, "How Do Teens Unwind?" The Gallup Organization (23 December 2003). http://www.gallup.com/poll/content/?ci = 10222&pg = 1 (accessed 18 July 2005).

8. Linda Lyons, "What Are Teens Doing After School?" The Gallup Organization (19 April 2005). http://www.gallup.com/poll/content/?ci = 15943&pg = 1 (accessed 18 July 2005).

9. Ibid.

10. www.biblehistory.com.

CHAPTER 3—PARTNER WITH OTHERS IN THE GOSPEL: TIMOTHY

1. "Barna Identifies Seven Paradoxes Regarding America's Faith," The Barna Group (17 December 2002). http://www.barna.org/FlexPage.aspx?Page = BarnaUpdate&BarnaUpdateID = 128 (accessed 19 July 2005).

2. "Are Short-Term Missions Good Stewardship?" Christianity Today (5 July 2005). http://www.christianitytoday.com/ct/2005/127/22.0.html (accessed 19 July 2005).

3. "Mission (Christian)," Wikipedia. http://en.wikipedia.org/wiki/Mission_%28Christian%29 (accessed 19 July 2005).

4. Kenneth S. Wuest, *Wuest's Word Studies from the Greek New Testament*, vol. 3 (Grand Rapids: Eerdmans, 1973).

CHAPTER 4—MAKE NO COMPROMISE: SHADRACH, MESCHACH, AND ABED-NEGO

1. Chris King, "Christian at Harvard Feels Culture Shock," *Orlando Sentinel* (3 July 2005). www.orlandosentinel.com/news/opinion/orl-inschrisking070305jul03,1,926958.story?coll = orl-opinion-utility (accessed 18 July 2005).

2. Ibid.

3. Matt Kaufman, "Fear of God at Harvard," Kaufman on Campus (1999). http://www.boundless.org/1999/regulars/kaufman/a0000095.html (accessed 19 July 2005).

4. Ibid.

5. Eric Langborgh, "Harvard Throws Christians to the Lions," Accuracy in Academia. (3 March 1999). http://www.academia.org/campus_reports/1999/march_1999_3.html (accessed 19 July 2005).

6. Ibid.

7. Chris King, "Christian at Harvard Feels Culture Shock."

8. "Religions Expression in Public Schools," U.S. Department of Education (May 1998). http://www.ed.gov/Speeches/08-1995/religion.html (accessed 18 July 2005).

9. Ibid.

10. Ibid.

11. "The Equal Access Act," U.S. Department of Education (May 1998). http://www.ed.gov/Speeches/08-1995/religion.html (accessed 18 July 2005).

12. Fuad Matar, *Saddam Hussein: A Biographical and Ideological Account of His Leadership Style and Crisis Management* (London: Highlight Publications, 1990 [originally published in 1979]), 235. See also Efraim Karsh and Inari Rautsi, *Saddam Hussein: A Political Biography* (New York: The Free Press, 1991), 122–23, 152–53, as reported at http://hnn.us/articles/1305.html.

CHAPTER 5—KEEP AN OPEN HEART: LYDIA

1. "Real Life," Simple Truth: Generation Next. http://www.simpletruth.org/myintouch/youth/teen/hangin_out/november/a_37183525.html (accessed 19 July 2005).

2. Elesha Hodge, "Close Encounters," *Campus Life* (1999 January/February). http://www.christianitytoday.com/cl/9c4/9c4024.html (accessed 19 July 2005).

3. Ibid.

4. Ibid.

5. "Jennifer Knapp," Christian Music Today. http://www.christianitytoday.com/music/artists/jenniferknapp.html (accessed 18 July 2005).

6. Ibid.

7. "Take Five," *Today's Christian Woman* (March/April 2003): 74.

8. "Evangelism Is Most Effective Among Kids," The Barna Group (11 October 2004). http://www.barna.org/FlexPage.aspx?Page = BarnaUpdate&BarnaUpdateID = 172 (accessed 7 July 2005).

9. "Teenagers Embrace Religion but Are Not Excited About Christianity," The Barna Group (10 January 2000). http://www.barna.org/FlexPage.aspx?Page = BarnaUpdate&BarnaUpdateID = 45 (accessed 7 July 2005).

10. "Americans are Most Likely to Base Truth on Feelings," The Barna Group (12 February 2002). http://www.barna.org/FlexPage.aspx?Page = BarnaUpdate&BarnaUpdateID = 106 (accessed 6 July 2005).

11. Ibid.

12. E. Barker, *The Making of a Moonie* (Oxford: Basil Blackwell, 1984), 147.

CHAPTER 6—KEEP THE DREAM ALIVE: JOSEPH

1. "Homeless to Harvard: The Liz Murray Story," Lifetime. http://www.lifetimetv.com/community/olc/cable/educational_homeless.html (accessed 19 July 2005).

2. Rachel Cohen, "Homeless to Harvard: Interview" Lifetime. http://www.lifetimetv.com/community/olc/hero/homeless_harvard3.html (accessed 19 July 2005).

3. Jon Dudas, "Welcome from Our Director," U.S. Patent and Trademark Office. http://www.uspto.gov/web/offices/ac/ahrpa/opa/kids/special/kidhello.html (accessed 19 July 2005).

4. Ibid.

5. Hillel Italie, "Books Abound but Buyers Don't," *Wisconsin State Journal* (17 May 2005). http://www.madison.com/wsj/home/biz/index.php?ntid = 40211&ntpid = 2 (accessed 19 July 2005).

6. Kamel, "Trader Tip Off Platinum Bond," Hollywood Stock Exchange (12 June 2001). http://www.hsx.com/community/trenches/010612.htm (accessed 19 July 2005).

7. Clarence Edward Macartney, *Preaching Without Notes* (New York: Abingdon-Cokesbury Press, 1946), 121–22.

8. Chuck Swindoll, *Great Lives in God's Word: Joseph* (Nashville: W Publishing, 1998), xi.

CHAPTER 7—TURN PAIN INTO COMPASSION: ESTHER

1. Lyons, Linda. "What Frightens America's Youth?" The Gallup Organization. (29 March 2005) 19 July 2005. http://www.gallup.com/poll/content/?ci = 15439&pg = 1

2. Ibid.

3. George H. Gallup Jr., "How Many Teens See Purpose for Life?" The Gallup Organization (6 April 2004). http://www.gallup.com/poll/content/?ci = 11215&pg = 1 (accessed 19 July 2005).

CHAPTER 8—START A REVOLUTION: JOHN THE BAPTIST

1. "Teenagers Embrace Religion but Are Not Excited About Christianity," The Barna Group (10 January 2000). http://www.barna.org/FlexPage.aspx?Page = BarnaUpdate&BarnaUpdateID = 45 (accessed 7 July 2005).

2. Cassie Moore, "Tips for Getting the Most from High School and College Students Who Volunteer," The Chronicle of Philanthropy (2 June 2004). http://philanthropy.com/jobs/2004/06/10/20040610-285129.htm (accessed 13 July 2005).

3. George H. Gallup Jr., "Teens Aim for the Simple Things In Life," The Gallup Organization (6 January 2004). http://www.gallup.com/poll/content/?ci = 10282&pg = 1 (accessed 14 July 2005).

4. Charles McComb, "Teens and Social Service: Who Volunteers?" The Gallup Organization (27 May 2003). http://www.gallup.com/poll/content/?ci = 8500&pg = 1 (accessed 14 July 2005).

ABOUT THE AUTHORS

Jay Strack, president and founder of Student Leadership University, is an inspiring and effective communicator, author, and minister. Acclaimed by leaders in the business world, religious affiliations, and education realms as a dynamic speaker, Jay has spoken to an estimated 15 million people in his 30 years of ministry. His versatile style has been presented across the country and in 22 countries, before government officials, corporate groups, numerous professional sports teams in the NFL, NBA, and MLB, to over 9,500 school assemblies, and at some 100 universities. Zig Ziglar calls Jay Strack, "entertaining, but powerful, inspiring and informative."

Ron Luce is the President and Founder of Teen Mania Ministries, a Christian youth organization that reaches millions of young people worldwide. Ron passionately declares the truth of the gospel without compromise as he challenges teenagers to take a stand for Christ in their schools, communities, and throughout the world. Raised in a broken home, Ron ran away from home at the age of 15 and became involved in drug and alcohol abuse before finding Jesus at the age of 16. The life-transforming impact of Christ inspired Ron to dedicate his life to reaching young people.

After receiving both bachelor's and master's degrees in counseling and psychology, Ron and his wife, Katie, started Teen Mania in 1986 with nothing more than a hatchback car and a dream to raise up an army of young people who would change the world. He has received an honorary doctorate from Liberty University and was appointed by President Bush to serve as an advisory member for the Commission and Drug free Communities in 2002—present.

Ron is a sought-after speaker who has traveled to more than 50 countries and has made numerous media appearances, such as Dr. James Dobson's Focus on the Family radio broadcast and The 700 Club. He is also a frequent host and guest on the Trinity Broadcasting Network. Ron and Katie live in Lindale, Texas with their three children, Hannah, Charity, and Cameron.

TEEN MANIA
MINISTRIES

Teen Mania is fighting for today's teens.

Teen Mania's heartbeat is to provoke a young generation to passionately pursue Jesus Christ and to take His life-giving message to the ends of the earth.

Founded in 1986 by Ron Luce, Teen Mania reaches teens through several primary outreaches:

  # Events

Held in approximately 30 cities across North America each year, Acquire the Fire events create an environment where teens' hearts are captured by God, and biblical truths are imparted through high-impact multimedia, live drama, music and teaching.

www.battlecry.com
(click on "Events")

 # Mission Trips

Global Expeditions is committed to bringing the Truth of Jesus Christ to the countless thousands around the world who are in desperate need of His love. Teens and leaders travel the world with Global Expeditions and bring the message of hope to the hopeless. Since its inception in 1986, Teen Mania has taken more than 40,000 teens around the world and documented over one million people who have committed their lives to Christ as a result.

www.globalexpeditions.com

 # Internship

The Honor Academy gives high school graduates an opportunity to impact the world for Christ while developing the character and leadership skills they need for life-long success. Interns are actively involved in all the ministries of Teen Mania. The scope of the program is extensive and includes classroom instruction, practical hands-on experience, and life-transforming events.

www.honoracademy.com

 # Media

The Center of Creative Media trains young innovators to connect their culture with the message of the gospel. CCM interns not only receive training from industry experts, they are also actively involved in producing media for live events, the Internet and broadcast. The Acquire the Fire TV show attracts approximately 400,000 viewers each week across North America, and many more in over 200 nations around the world.

www.centerforcreativemedia.com

Lead, follow or be bait.
This is where the journey begins – SLU101!
At Student Leadership University, you won't find canoes and campfires. What you will find is a 4-day comprehensive program designed to catapult you into a life of confidence, significance, and leadership. SLU prepares you to successfully navigate the shark-infested waters of our culture with the rules and tools of leadership. Stop hanging out with the bait fish. Come to SLU where dreaming is encouraged and the language of leadership is spoken freely.
Explore the possibilities at
www.studentleadership.net
Student Leadership University

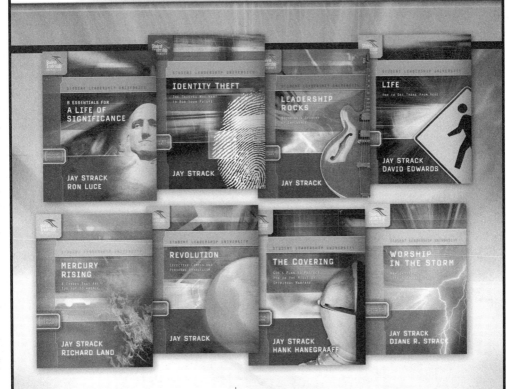